The

MW01288628

of Cookery :

Recipes For a Delighted Tongue, a Healthy Body and a Magical Life

The Silver Elves

DEDICATION

This book is dedicated to:

Silver Flame's mother, Martha, and Zardoa's father, Joseph, who were both great cooks.

Witches say: "If you can't fly with the Big Girls, then stay off the broom."

We elves say: "If you can't dance with wee folk, then stay out of the Circle." This is so for we must always look out for the little folk. This book is written for all our little folk who we ever seek to nourish and nurture.

TABLE OF CONTENTS

It is important to remember to smile and sing and laugh and have positive thoughts while you cook! The food will carry your life energy and good wishes to help nurture all who eat it. And most certainly do swallow your smiles often as you cook to bring happiness to your own gut!

A Note from the Silver Elves

You will note little enchantments or spells here and there throughout the book that can be chanted when cooking to fill a dish with that special elfin magick. We cook consciously and with healing intent.

My cooking spoon

My magic wand

Of this dish

You'll be fond!

Wealthy, Healthy, Lucky too,

Are those who eat this wondrous brew.

Each spice and herb that I do add

Will make your heart rejoice, be glad!

Awaken magic in the soul

Of those who eat and are made whole.

Healing Magic I instill

Far greater this

Than any pill!

Soothing, calming easy be,

Your energy is now set free!

Triple, triple

Outward ripple

From head to toe

And thigh to nipple.

Filling now with Light and Magic

Banishing all that's sad and tragic.

Every bite will us unite

Our lives with love and Light.

I mix, I stir, I blend, I grind

And all I wish I soon will find!

Bake, bake, bake

The Truth will reveal

All that is

Fake, fake, fake.

Each bite we take doth taste right

And brings to each a guiding Light.

Troubles will all fade away

As this bakes and saves the day!

Nether Realms Double Chocolate Cherry Cookies (see page 94)

Introduction

There are over 50 original recipes in this book and all are very delicious and healthy foods—many entire meals. The recipes that we have included are from our personal collection of elven recipes that we have created over a 40-year span of time and that we have refined to healthy versions for gut and heart over the years to reflect modern knowledge about excellent nutrition and well-being.

Best of all in this book, you will be given cooking tips throughout that will help you become a skilled and creative cook with gut and heart health in mind. Once you have learned these 50+ recipes, you will have not only a great daily diet, but also the ability to make up your own variations of a large selection of types of dishes and alter any recipe you find on the internet or otherwise into a healthy but very tasty version of your own elven cooking that will serve your specific dietary needs.

This book is not only an elven recipe book, but also a course in how to cook and to alter recipes to your health specifications. Reading this book will demonstrate to you, for instance, how to take an old family recipe of your own mother's and make changes to it that render it healthier—and yet satisfy your yearning for the comfort of her cooking (more on that in Chapter 2). Furthermore, many of those delicious looking recipes you come across while surfing the web can be altered to a more healthy version for heart and gut and you will find some of these also included in this book.

You are also encouraged to alter the recipes in this book even further, to accommodate your own health concerns and the latest diet information and research past the time of writing this book. While we have added as much dietary knowledge and resources as possible for you to use, in determining what are healthy ingredients for you specifically, it is advised to go over you particular needs with your health care physician.

So, time to cook and eat creatively and to make your food preparation a part of your life art and magic.

A Note on Elven Cookery

In our experience, the most contentious issue on ListServes and discussion groups on the Internet concerning and among Elves, Faeries and Otherkin always concerned the debate about vegetarianism versus meat eating. Our view has always been and continues to be that as we evolve as soulful spirits we will tend toward more and more subtle and energetic foods and tend away from foods that involve violence and killing. We know that others disagree with this view and while we don't share their opinion we acknowledge their right to hold it. While these elves tend to be vegetarian, we do not say that all elves should or must be. Each spirit must determine its own path.

We were primarily trained and initiated into the various Elven magical arts by the Elf Queen's Daughters. These sisters always emphasized to us that the Law of Community topped the Law of Dietary Restrictions. By this they meant that if one visited another family or tribe and one was offered meat by them, even if one was vegetarian, the elf/elves ate the meat offered, certainly blessing the animal that provided its life. Of course this Law is restricted within reason of one's personal medical needs.

We have added to this the idea that the Law of Individual Need and Aspiration tops the Law of Community, thus while we will eat meat if offered by our host, we make no demands on our guests to eat as we do. In fact, in our elven home we seek to adapt to the tastes and needs of each one who lives with us or comes to us. The choice about being vegetarian or not is an individual soulful choice and whatever the choice may be, we respect it and adapt to it. Thus among the many vegetarian recipes you will find in this book you will always find a few involving meat or fish. Of course, meat substitutes are available in most food stores. And naturally, if meat or fish is your favored food you can adapt many of these recipes by adding either of them.

However, while elves may disagree on whether the elven as a people are essentially vegetarian or not, most elves can agree that elven food has two essential aspects. The first is taste and the second is nutrition. Elven food must be tasty and healthy. We do not sacrifice one for the other, although the second in our mind is more important than the first. Still, as we have observed, while it may be more important to eat healthy food than to eat tasty food, it is unlikely that one will continue to do so if that food is not delicious. We elves are aware that we are not only feeding the body but the soulful spirit as well.

Thus we created this book for all elves to adapt to their own needs both healthy and flavorful. We have made and eaten all the recipes ours'elves and continue to adapt them according to our tastes, our understanding of nutrition and what we may have in the cupboard on a particular day. We trust you will do the same, making this your own book of magical elven recipes.

A Few Words About
The Elven Body Type

Stories and fairy tales about elf folk frequently indicate that our kin are both thin and athletic. You very seldom read reference to fat elves. However, it should be noted that we elves make no prohibitions concerning a person's weight or size. Our concern is ever that an individual should be happy, in as much as possible with their own appearance; and, as stated previously, that they eat in such a way as to promote good health, vitality and spiritual well being.

However, while we offer healthy recipes, diet isn't just about nutrition but also moderation, exercise and balance. Each elf needs to decide for hir own s'elf what is best for hir (him/her) and what will further hir spirit and evolutionary development as a soul. Just as elves, and others, may disagree on what is tasty and flavorful, adapting these recipes to one's own taste, so too each elf must decide for hir own s'elf what is healthy for hir spirit, soul and body. Still, it is our experience that among elves if one truly loves ones'elf, other elves will love you as well, just the way you are whether you be tall or short, thin or not so svelte. It is the spirit elves tend to see and judge by, much more than the physical appearance. We see what lies beneath and beyond. We are well aware of being eternal spirits in transitory bodies, but we do not despise the body, as many religions seem to do, rather we see the body as our vehicle of manifestation. Just like any other vehicle: plane, car, or bicycle, it is best to keep it well maintained and in prime operating condition. We elves are not here to escape the material world but to master it by mastering our own s'elves and our magic.

A Word About "Elf Notes and Tips"

Most of the tips in the *Elf Notes and Tips* sections are important things to know that will make your cooking experience go more smoothly. Many we learned from our own mothers, others from research and most from trial and discovery in our own kitchen. You will also occasionally find a little survival tip to help you plan ahead in your own kitchen for the unexpected loss of electricity or water during a storm or other disturbances in the Force.

In the beginning of the book, for the first few recipes, you will find more *Elf Notes and Tips* than in the later chapters of the book. This is to help you get started if you are a beginner. Still, do read them even if you have been cooking a while, because some of them will save you time and trouble. For instance, in the recipe on cooking a lemon cake with a lemon glaze, we give you a tip on how to keep your glazes and other fillings from globbing up horribly when a recipe calls for adding cornstarch to mixtures that need to boil in order to thicken. We have ruined a few berry pie fillings before learning this tip.

> *Health, Health, Wealth, Wealth*
>
> *Self, Self, Unlimited Be.*

And A Word About Tasting

It might as well be mentioned here before we go any further in our discussion of ingredient substitutions and cooking: You are encouraged to taste all along as you cook (just use a clean spoon for each taste)! We usually have about half a dozen clean spoons out ready on a plate to the side on the counter during any cooking spree in which we engage. It is important to learn to cook by taste (sight, touch, hearing, and smell, too) and obviously you need to be prepared to do some tasting when you cook! It is like learning to play music. The concert pianist who reads advanced musical notation also listens to every note. Cooking by following a recipe and not tasting until after you finish cooking would be like making a musical recording and not listening to what you were playing until after it was all recorded. Just as a fine musician listens as sHe (she/he) plays, the best cooks taste as they cook.

Updates and Recipe Versions

Here and there and at the end of some chapters, we have left some room with lines for you to write in your own notes. Please use these spaces to make notes to revise our recipes to your taste and adjust any recipe with which you experiment and find better versions for you. Also, write in your favorite recipes! And remember that new nutrition and dieting information is coming out all the time and you have to get actively involved in experimenting and changing your own recipes to accommodate these insights. We also would enjoy receiving from you any nutruitional updates you make on the recipes in this book and invite you to email us at silverelves@live.com.

❧

Here are two ancient elven spells used during cooking to increase wisdom and happiness and banish sadness. Use them freely and make up your own:

Take a bite and you will find
Wisdom of the heart and mind.

Every taste will bring your way
Happiness in all you say.

Chapter 1:
Changing a Recipe to Your Taste and to the Most Updated Knowledge About a Healthy Diet

It is important to view a recipe book as one that you use daily and what we in our family call "a living book"—a book that you use all the time, not just read once and disgard on the shelf. It is in a sense a spell book, a book of magical enchantments, to be consulted, used and altered as needed. We are elven witches around a cauldron brewing up concoctions that will transform the body toward great health and the soul toward greater joy and delight in life thus nurturing both the body and the spirit. And since using a cookbook is a continuing lifetime process, we urge you to experiment with your own recipes, adding your newest knowledge of diet and good healthy choices to your cooking. Please take our recipes and change them for the better for you and do this as often as you feel a need to do so. Experiment and have fun with it and make it constantly better! We do. We have even left you a few blank pages to work in so you can think of this book as a workbook to write in and really use, putting your own health needs into your creations.

The image of witches stirring a Cauldron, as in Shakespeare's Scottish play and of wizards and alchemists putting together potions for spells speaks to how deep, profound and ancient this magic of cookery is. In fact, one of the four treasures of the Tuatha de Danaan was the Cauldron of the Dagda from which none ever left unsatisfied. Cooking magic, nutritional magic, is at the heart of shamanism, alchemy and chemistry and its effects are so much more profound and lasting than that of wizards casting lighting at each other. Who doesn't carry within them the memory of home cooking? Only those who have missed out on something truly great, enriching and profound!

In this chapter, we will give you a few cooking tips and cooking chemistry principles for making ingredient substitutions that we have learned (some the disastrous hard way) and we hope they will help you in your revisions and improvements of our recipes, as well as for those recipes that you find elsewhere and wish to improve upon.

Each bite will bring a true delight

And every problem be set right.

Making Substitutions in Recipes

FLOUR SUBSTITUTIONS

For every 1 cup of white flour called for in a recipe, substitute 7/8 cup of organic whole wheat or try using organic sprouted whole grain flour. You will find in this book that we generally list whole wheat flour rather than sprouted whole grain flour because we find it difficult to get the latter on a regular basis. We have on occasion found it at Whole Foods, but not on a regular basis. We do use it, however, when we can get it because it has a higher nutritional value and is more easily digested than whole wheat. When you substitute sprouted wheat flours, remember that it has a higher absorption rate than regular flours, so add 1 tablespoon of liquid (water) per cup of flour to the original recipe that you are altering.

Also you may try swapping out 1 cup of whole wheat flour for 1 cup kinako (roasted soy bean) flour or white bean flour (navy bean) to add extra protein in your baked goods as well as cutting down on the gluten. Also, experiment with fava bean flour and garbanzo bean flour for some dishes. Bob's Red Mill makes a great gluten free All Purpose Baking Flour that uses the main ingredient as garbanzo beans. We usually don't add but 1 cup of bean flour to a recipe (and we prefer white bean flour because navy beans are more alkaline than most beans) that calls for 3 cups flour altogether (so about 1 to 3 ratio) because we find it overwhelms the taste of the baked good. You will need to experiment with this to suit your palette.

Also, for adding extra protein content in food, when baking breads, and particularly cookies and muffins (even pie crusts), experiment with nut flours like almond flour (ground blanched almonds) to add more protein to balance the more carbohydrate grain flours. We try to keep the ratio of carbohydrate to protein as close to 1 to 1 as possible (with 1 cup grain flour to 1 cup nut and/or bean flour). Almond flour is also used as a thickener and we often use it if we are also substituting in some fine flour like brown rice flour. Almond flour is a little sweet so it is delicious in baking cookies and muffins, and a real plus is that almonds are also alkaline. Cashew or pistachio flours are nice for desserts as well and add to the overall protein count.

Don't forget that you can add alternative grain flours too that are higher in protein than wheat flours. If you are allergic to wheat, are gluten intolerant, or just would like to use a variety of grains to increase protein and other nutritional value of your baked goods, here are eight of our favorite grain flours that may be substituted for part or all of the whole wheat flour called for in a recipe:

1. Quinoa flour is highly nutritious with more protein, calcium and iron than other grain flours. Has a nice nutty taste. We do not use it

alone and have found it best when substituting no more than $1/2^{th}$ cup Quinoa for $1/2^{th}$ cup wheat flour per recipe.

2. Kamut® is an ancient type of wheat related to the modernly used durum variety. Compared to regular whole wheat, Kamut® is richer in protein, vitamins, minerals, and unsaturated fatty acids. The down side is that it contains a little less dietary fiber. Kamut® flour has a mild and rather sweet taste. It can be substituted cup for cup for whole wheat in baking.

3. Buckwheat flour is considered gluten-free. It has a robust flavor. We often substitute a cup of buckwheat for 1 cup of wheat flour in a recipe. Be sure and add extra spices when you cook with Buckwheat as it can overwhelm the flavor if you do not add more. When we make ginger bread (which Zardoa loves) and use some Buckwheat, we always add lots of extra ginger. Buckwheat makes a very wholesome and delicious bread!

4. Millet flour is ground from millet seeds and is gluten-free with a buttery, sweet taste. It is high in vitamins and minerals. But because it can be a little grainy, we only substitute about ¼ millet flour for ¼ wheat flour per recipe (in other words, a little goes a long way).

5. Spelt flour (we like the white spelt variety) has a mild nutty flavor and is high in protein but low

in gluten. It is our favorite to use in substituting for wheat flour in making bread for those who are somewhat gluten and wheat intolerant. (One important note: Celiac patients find they may also be intolerant of Spelt flour.)

6. Amaranth flour is gluten-free and has a sweet taste. We often use it with whole wheat 1 to 1 in a recipe, that is half Amaranth and half whole wheat flour, although it also can be substituted cup for cup in a whole wheat recipe and teams well with buckwheat flour.

7. Coconut flour is very high in fiber. It is low in carbohydrates and a high in protein. It gives baked goods a rich flavor but it needs a lot more liquid than other flours. Replace no more than 1/3 of the flour called for in a recipe with coconut flour, and be sure and add an equivalent amount of additional liquid (water if none called for) to the recipe. Another positive for using it is that you will not need as much sweetener when using this flour because the coconut flour has a natural sweet taste.

Oat Flour is an excellent source of fiber and adds a rich sweetness to your baked goods. Bob's Red Mill has recently added certified gluten-free oats to its line of gluten-free products. We like to grind our own, using organic rolled oats in a coffee grinder, and find it can be substituted for at least half of the flour in a recipe calling for wheat. It is a must in any homemade bread!

Each of these flours absorbs water differently and some flours have a particularly strong taste—like quinoa flour—so you want to use only small amounts in your recipe.

Most of our recipes are not gluten-free as our family does not have a problem with gluten, but you can easily make gluten-free substitutions using the information above. White spelt and kamut flours are our substitutions of choice when we do cook for those who need gluten free food.

BASIC GLUTEN FREE BAKING FLOUR MIX

Here is a good basic gluten free baking flour mix you can use to substitute in any baking recipe instead of wheat flour. If you would like a gluten free food, try substituting it in any of our recipes in this book that call for whole wheat flour:

1 cup certified gluten free organic millet flour (or sorghum flour or certified gluten free oat flour)

1/2 cup organic almond meal flour

1 cup potato starch

1 teaspoon xanthan gum

You can also substitute other heavy flours instead of the almond flour. But be careful as these other flours including buckwheat, coconut, or quinoa flour will result in a denser food if you add too much to the overall recipe. Half cup of any of these flours is best in your flour blend.

For a self-rising flour, use 1 cup of the above flour blend recipe, 1 1/2 teaspoons baking powder and 2 pinches of Himalayan salt.

SUBSTITUTING LIQUIDS FOR DRY INGREDIENTS

When you substitute a liquid ingredient for a dry ingredient, be sure and reduce the other liquid ingredients in the recipe. That makes sense, right? For instance, you can substitute unsweetened applesauce for sugar in a 1 to 1 ratio. However, for every 1 cup of applesauce you use instead of sugar, just be sure and also reduce the amount of other liquids in the recipe by 1/4 cup for every cup of substituted applesauce (since it adds liquid to the recipe when sugar does not).

Another example of liquid for dry that we use quite a bit is organic raw agave or honey to substitute for sugar cane, and here because of the thickness of agave you do not need to worry so much about cutting down on some other liquid ingredient but you certainly can add less agave than sugar (because agave is sweeter than sugar). We generally add ¾ cup of agave instead of 1 cup of sugar. It's up to your taste.

Although raw organic agave syrup has a lower glycemic index than sugar, remember that it is primarily fructose and glucose. And thus must be processed through your liver like alcohol. The organic raw agave is less processed, uses lower heat and less time cooking for processing, than the regular agave (not raw) but it is still to be used with caution and as little as possible. Also, in thinking of nutrient density, it is important to remember that the micronutrient content of agave nectar is low but it does contain cancer fighting saponins & inulin.

We also suggest substituting 1 teaspoon Stevia powder plus ¼ cup agave or honey to equal ½ cup sugar cane in any of our recipes. This formula is low glycemic and has no Stevia bad after taste.

A WORD ABOUT EGG REPLACEMENT

If eggs are a problem for you, then for two average eggs, combine: 1 tablespoon Ener-G Egg Replacer and 4 tablespoons water (filtered and warm). Whip it up and although it does not blend well, it will work in your baking. You might also try leaving out the egg and add an extra teaspoon of baking powder (along with a couple of tablespoons of almond milk to replace the liquid of the egg). We have done this when we were out of eggs and it worked fine.

Three Important Healthy Ways to Alter and Improve a Recipe

Besides using all non-GMO food ingredients without use of pesticides or artificial additives and also using organic and local foods whenever possible as well as an almost exclusive use of healthy omega-3 olive oil in all cooking, there are three health improving goals that we try to maintain for each recipe we alter. These three are (all three combined will aid both your gut and heart health): 1. Increase Nutrient Density 2. Lower the Glycemic Index 3. Maintain a slightly alkaline pH Balance. You may have other criteria for your recipes, but these three seem to be the most important to our own health and to what we have found for our family and friends in maintaining a happy gut and healthy heart. Although we have already discussed some things to do to meet these criteria, let's take a look at these one by one.

Adding Ingredients for Nutrient Density

In all your cooking, try to add as many ingredients that are high in a variety of nutrients and cut out (make substitutions of higher nutritional value) ingredients that have little to no nutritional value, like white flour and white sugar. You are looking to make everything that goes in your mouth as "nutrient dense" as possible (am not sure who first coined this phrase but we like it). Treat your snacks the same way, make them add to your nutritional richness count for the day and not just be for eating fun (although eating needs to be pleasurable as well). This means not just eliminating nutrient poor foods like sugar and white flour, but also adding extra beneficial nutrients. Both of these steps are important—eliminating poor nutrient foods and adding nutrient rich foods. If you are cooking for someone who will not eat food without the use of the poor nutrient foods, you can at least add nutrient rich ingredients into your cooking (we'll be sharing some of our own secrets in doing that without the dinner guest you are cooking for knowing you have "naturally nutrient enriched" their food).

But you may be asking, "What foods are highest in nutrient density?" Dr. Joel Furhman (see his book **"*Eat for Health*")** created the Aggregate Nutrient Density Index or the ANDI, which is a score assigned to whole foods that contain the highest nutrients per calorie and are the foods from which our bodies are able to absorb and utilize the most nutrients. The ANDI Score goes from 1 to 1000 with 1 being sodas and 1000 being Kale and Collards (so the higher score the better). You may have guessed this, but some of the other scores may surprise you. For instance, eating a Tomato is higher in ANDI than eating an Apple and eating French Fries is less nutritious than eating Vanilla Ice cream.

It is important to eat a variety of top ANDI super foods (as different food contain different nutrients) to get all the many nutrients your body needs. Here is a list of the top nutritionally rich foods according to Dr. Joel Fuhrman's ANDI scoring system:

Kale, Collard Greens, Watercress, Bok Choy, Spinach, Broccoli, Cabbage, Brussels Sprouts, Swiss Chard, Arugula, Mustard Greens, and Parsley.

For comparison sake, look at this list of food and ANDI scores (see Appendix 1 in the back of this book) and you will see that it is important to eat as much as possible from raw leafy green vegetables and solid green vegetables, then other non-green and non starchy vegetables, then from legumes and beans, then from fresh fruits, then starchy vegetables, then whole grains, then raw seeds and nuts, then fish, then fat free dairy, then wild meats and fowl, then eggs, then red meat, then dairy (not fat free), then cheese, then refined grain, then refined oils, and last refined sweets.

Obviously, we must pick some foods from the lower nutrient density scores or we would not have enough fat in our diets (but let's make them the healthiest possible like olive oil with high levels of monounsaturated), or avocado, coconut and sesame seed oils for cooking are also other omega healthy oils. Remember that monounsaturated oils help lower LDL (bad) cholesterol while also boosting HDL (good) cholesterol. And avocado oil is particularly suggested for baking because it can withstand high temperatures without being degraded.

We also must take advantage of what food is available in organics and locally grown, as these are higher in nutritional value than non-organics or food shipped long distances to us losing their nutritional value over the long haul of shipping time. So the ANDI score is not the only thing we have to look at in choosing our over all diet. But, reading the list in Appendix 1 before you go to the grocery store will help you remember the majority of potent super foods you wish to purchase to eat before being bombarded with ads of food products with very low nutritional value.

> Hint: Take this book with you to the grocery store as a reference for ANDI scores and healthy ingredients!

LOWERING THE GLYCEMIC INDEX

In our recipes, we use organic raw agave instead of cane sugar because it is lowest of the sweeteners on the glycemic index. We also suggest raw honey as an alternative because it has some nutritional values although higher on the glycemic index than agave. Also, we tend to make cookies and cakes that are not so sweet as the typical store bought ones, again as a consequence of less sugars used. Whenever possible, we also use fruits as natural sweeteners, like raisins, as they are both nutritious (whereas cane sugar for instance has no food value) and lower on the glycemic index than other sweeteners. Also, the glycemic index is lower in whole grains than processed flours, so you will find all flours in the recipes in this book are whole grains.

Because adding protein ingredients to carbohydrate ingredients lowers the glycemic index of the food, we also have tried to keep as close to at least a 50-50 balance of carbohydrate-to-protein balance in foods as possible. You will find in most of our recipes, we use an abundance of ingredients high in protein for baking, like omega-3 eggs, nut flours and nut milk, chopped whole nuts and seeds as ingredients in carbohydrates and sweets like cakes, cookies and muffins. This improves nutrient density but also helps to balance the carbohydrate-to-protein ratio and lowers the glycemic index of the food.

BALANCING YOUR ACID-ALKALINE pH LEVELS

Much has been written about the importance of balancing our pH levels. Diets high in processed foods give us highly acidic pH levels that have been linked to contributing both to gut and heart diseases, as well as cancer. We suggest that you buy some pH testing tape at your local health food store and regularly test your saliva and urine to determine if your levels are balanced.

While experts do not always agree on which foods are alkaline and which are acidic, we have made a chart you will find in Appendix 2 that will give you the basic agreement by cross referencing several experts who test for pH levels of food once they enter the body. Some lists you may find on the Internet will be different because they show the pH of foods outside the body. Lemons and limes for instance are acidic outside the body but turn alkaline inside the body. We are only interested here in what happens to our food once it enters our bodies.

The rule of thumb by most dietary experts is to try to have ¾ of your food and drinks on the alkaline side and only ¼ acidic. A neutral pH level is around 7, with lower being more acidic and higher more alkaline. We have tried to make the food in this book as balanced in pH levels as possible and a little to the alkaline side whenever possible. We suggest that you test your body pH with the pH tape early morning to determine how you are doing on this as you experiment with the recipes in this book and as you create your own recipes.

Hint: Remember that green tea is more alkaline, so drink it in between or to substitute the consumption of your coffee and regular black tea, along with plenty of filtered water with a little fresh lemon juice. And another wonderful alkaline non-caffeine herbal tea that is excellent in your chalice both hot or cold is organic nettle leaf tea.

Chapter Summary

All that being said about what we should be eating the most in our diets, you will find many of the recipes in this book are from the foods that you should have less often—baked goods like cookies and muffins. But, we all need variety and enjoyment of taste in our diets. So we have concentrated on "healthy sweets" that are not too high in sugar content (low as possible on the glycemic index) but are high as possible in nutrient density due to selected ingredient inclusions including super foods, and have a fairly balanced pH level. Eat these in moderation and enjoy excellent health.

From the source

The magic flows

And all I wish to be

Quickly grows.

Your Own Notes and Spells Go Here:

_____

_____

_____

_____

_____

_____

Chapter 2:
Altering Dishes

You probably think as we do that your Mom was a great cook (or in Zardoa's case, his Dad) and you may even be lucky enough to have some of her favorite recipes written down somewhere. Although your Mom may have been a wonderful cook and did not have you eating at fast food restraurants like seems to be hurting many people with that habit today, her recipes may not be exactly what you now know to be healthy, nutritionally speaking. Problem may be, when she was a cook in her day, no one knew what they know now about nutrition. Oil was oil and no one cared if it was "good oil" or "bad oil", saturated or not, while granulated sugar was mostly in desserts, it wasn't seen as so bad for your health as it is today, and there was no awareness that there is such a thing as too much salt in the diet. Mom may have been a cook before refined flour was known to turn to paste in your stomach, causing digestion problems and deteriation of health—in fact, pre-sifted white flour was considered a revered modern convenience in the 50s and 60s. Today, many of us have family and friends we may be cooking for that are struggling with illnesses like diabetes, digestive diseases, heart disease, high blood pressure, liver disease, or cancer that require special dietary concerns that must be taken in account in recipe ingredients. And of course we want to eat as healthily as possible ourselves and certainly we wish to provide a healthy diet for our children and grandchildren. Still, we can use many of our mom's recipes and simply make some healthy substitutions. It isn't hard to invent altered and more healthy recipes from your mom's cooking, because you know how it is suppose to taste (who could ever forget mom's cooking?). You can keep experimenting with new healthier ingredients until you make the recipe taste like your mom's (at least almost) but healthier. We're going to work on that in this book.

Where to Start In Making Healthy Substitutions

Before we begin cooking for our friends and relatives with special ingredient needs due to illness or specific body food requirements from food allergies or age, we make four lists of foods. The first list has all the foods on it that are "Absolutely No, Do not Eat" for this person. It can be pretty long. The second list has all the foods that can be eaten moderately. We usually make a little note next to each food item as to how often it can be eaten (once a week, once a month, once every 3 months, once or twice a year). Then the third list is of all the foods that are on the "Yes You Can" list and these are the foods that can be eaten by this person in abundance, even every day is fine for many on this list and you can add a star next to those. This list is the one you want to go out of your way to develop and even add new foods to that list that the person may not have previously tried. The fourth list is of foods that should be eaten as "Much as Possible" for the health of this particular person. These may come from your third list and be the ones with the star by them. Also add any foods that this person does not presently eat but would be helpful for them to eat for their particular medical condition. Be sure and add herbs and spices and foods like chia seeds and flax meal to your four lists. Make these 4 lists for all the people you cook for in your elven family.

You will find that we use some ingredients over and over in our recipes. This is because they are ones that we have determined in our family are the most healthy for our gut and heart health and on our 3rd or 4th lists, "Yes You Can" or even some on the "As Much as Possible", including: organic olive oil, organic flax seed meal, chia seed meal, avocado, whole grains, Greek Yogurt, almonds, almond meal and almond milk, pine nuts, garlic, onions, shitake mushrooms, raw spinach, organic tomatoes, pumpkin, celery, kale, broccoli, whole grains, raisins, blueberries and island fruit.

Making these lists can be time consuming but it is extremely important in cooking for a loved one with an illness or need that requires ingredient concerns. And it is your task to make food that is healthy as well as tasty and is an alternative for healing and well-being. Now you are ready to experiment with cooking healthy foods for the people you love by making substitutions in recipes. Just follow the dos and don'ts of your lists, read on, and use your imagination!

What to Do When you Yearn for "Unhealthy Comfort Foods"

What do you do when you yearn for comfort food—a piece of your mother's cherry pie or one of her old time most delicious dinners—but you have dietary concerns about some of the ingredients her recipes call for? Simple, you just experiment making healthy substitutions to her original recipe. One of the purposes of this book is to help you be able to recover and convert your own mom's dishes into amazing dishes that will satisfy your longing for her cooking and be good for your well-being at the same time. And if you are a caregiver for a friend or family member with special dietary concerns, these substitution tips and recipes will help you alter your loved ones favorite dishes as well.

To demonstrate how to make one of these cooking conversions of your mother's old recipes, we are going to give you a couple of examples from Silver Flame's own mother's delicious recipes that we have changed with healthy substitutions, yet have kept the wonderful flavor and great taste just like her mother made (well almost). When she was 90 years old, she wrote down all of Silver Flame's favorite recipes that she would cook for her as a child and sent them to us. In this chapter, we have shared two of Silver Flame's childhood favorites of her mother's recipes, first in original form as she cooked it and then followed by our modern altered version of her original recipe made with healthy substitutes.

Emotions and Need for Comfort Foods

One of the most diffiult things a person has to go through when first diagnosed with an illness, is to change their diet. Many people have said that it feels like "punishment" that they now can not eat certain foods that had given them a feeling of comfort. Much of our foods that we suddenly find ourselves having to cut out or limit are foods we have been eating from childhood and remind us of the comfort of "dear mom" or grannie or auntie or deceased spouse or from some other comforting person or place like our favorite restaurant or bakery. That is why learning to take some of your mom's dishes or other dishes you have had in your diet for comfort (pastries for instance) and alter them to heart healthy, low glycemic and dense nutrient foods is so important.

RECIPE FOR: Shrimp & Rice
FROM THE KITCHEN OF: mcw p.19
PAGE 350°

1/4 pstr or 4 oz can sliced mushrooms
2 Tbles butter
1 lb shrimp cooked
3 C. cooked white rice
1 1/2 C shredded sharp cheddar cheese
1/2 C Half & Half
2 T catsup
1 tsp. worcestershire sauce
dash of fresh ground pepper

Drain Mushrooms reserve liquid - Saute mush. in Butter about 10 min. Mix lightly with shrimp, rice & cheese.
Combine cream, catsup, Worcestershire & pepper add to rice mixture.
Bake in a buttered casserole for approx 25-30 min. 350° oven
Use mushroom liquid if mixture is a bit dry, depending on how moist rice is.
mcw

Above: Original recipe from the kitchen of Martha Campbell Whitenton. When Silver Flame's mother, Martha Campbell Whitenton, was 90 years old, she wrote out all of Silver Flame's favorite childhood recipes and sent them to us. Chapter 3 will show you one way to alter this recipe to make it healthier and yet still have the flavor goodness of mom's cooking.

Chapter 3:
How We Altered
Two of Mother's Recipes

Recipe 1: Mother's Original Shrimp and Rice Dish

Ingredients:

4 oz. can sliced or ¼ cup fresh mushrooms

2 tablespoons oleo or butter

2 tablespoons catsup

1 lb. shrimp cooked

3 cups cooked white rice

1½ cups shredded sharp cheddar cheese

½ cup half and half

1 teaspoon Worcestershire Sauce

dash of fresh ground pepper

Steps for Making Shrimp and Rice Dish:

1. Drain mushrooms, reserve liquid and sauté

mushrooms in butter about 10 minutes. Mix lightly with shrimp you have pre-cooked (the shrimp is pre-cooked by peeling, and then boiling for 10 minutes in enough water to amply cover the shrimp, then draining off water).

2. Add in rice and cheese.

3. Combine half and half cream, catsup, Worcestershire Sauce and pepper.

6. Add to the rice and shrimp mixture.

7. Bake in a buttered casserole in oven for approximately 25-30 minutes at 350 degrees. Use mushroom liquid if mixture is a bit dry, depending on how moist the rice is.

Our Altered Healthy Version of Silver Flame's Mother's Shrimp and Rice Dish

Silver Flame was nervous to do this revision at first, thinking she might be really making a mess of one of her mother's favorite dishes. But there is really nothing that will prime the well of making you into a superior cook like stepping in your own mother's apron in the kitchen and even going an extra few steps beyond her efforts. So grab your apron and remember that she would most likely be happy you helped make her recipes live on in your life, even if the form changes a bit to make them even more healthy for you. Although there is a difference in the two versions of this shrimp dish, the unusual combination of ingredients makes this dish uniquely have the flavor of Silver Flame's mother's cooking in whatever version we alter it.

Ingredients:

4 tablespoons chopped fresh organic shitake mushrooms

2 tablespoons organic olive oil

2 tablespoons organic raw agave catsup (see recipe in chapter 9 for making your own catsup)

1 lb. shrimp cooked and then peeled (use wild caught from US and British Columbia, sustainably caught, or buy farm shrimp with Best Aquaculture Practices label, raised without antibiotics)

3 cups cooked organic short grain brown rice

1½ cups shredded organic extra sharp cheddar cheese (certified non-GMO)

½ cup organic nonfat dry milk mixture (add 3 tablespoons dry milk mixture powder to ½ cup (4 oz.) cold water and stir well)

2 to 3 teaspoon organic Worcestershire sauce
(we increased the amount because brown
rice needs more flavoring than white)

dash of fresh ground pepper

(optional) 2 teaspoons kelp powder

(optional) We also like it with one garlic bulb
that is chopped and sautéed with the
mushrooms

(optional) Sometimes, we like to add 1/8 cup
pine nuts on top after it is cooked,

although we advise you to make it the
first time without them and them give
them a try if it seems like your palette
would go for it.

(optional) ¼ cup shredded cheese to sprinkle
on top the last 3 minutes in the oven.

Steps for Making Silver Flame's Version of Mother's Shrimp and Rice Dish:

1. Drain mushrooms, reserve liquid and sauté mushrooms in olive oil about 7 minutes. Add kelp to mushrooms. Mix lightly with shrimp (the shrimp is

pre cooked by peeling, and then boiling for 10 minutes in enough water to amply cover the shrimp, then drained of water).

2. Add in brown rice and cheese. Combine the dry milk mixture, catsup, Worcestershire Sauce and pepper. Add to the rice and shrimp mixture.

3. Bake in a casserole dish oiled with olive oil in the oven for approximately 25-30 minutes at 350 degrees. Use mushroom liquid if mixture is a bit dry, depending on how moist the rice is.

This makes enough for 6 servings. As this is primarily a protein dish, serve it with one or two vegetables on the plate and a green salad on the side! We like it with baked Okinawan sweet potatoes and steamed green beans as side dishes.

A word about the cheese and cream in this recipe: We have tried, for those in my family who cannot eat dairy, to alter this recipe with almond cheese and almond milk instead of cheese and cream. While when using almond instead of milk products we were not successful in making a dish that replicates the sumptuous flavor of Silver Flame's mother's original dish, it was still quite splendid. And those who have served it to have raved how good it was (of course, they had not ever tasted Mother's original recipe to compare). The original dish really requires a sharp cheese for full flavor (and it is even hard to find an organic one that is sharp enough to really work well). So if your dietary concerns limit you to almond milk and cheese substitutions, we recommend you experiment adding other ingredients for extra flavor, like garlic, and you are sure to create a new and healthy dish you and those you cook for will love.

❧

Recipe 2: Mother's Saving Grace Spaghetti

As a small child, Silver Flame would not eat and the doctor told her parents that she would starve if they could not get her to eat something—anything would be fine. There was one thing she would eat and so they fed it to her almost every day—spaghetti! Silver Flame's mother's spaghetti literally saved her from starvation, thus the name Saving Grace Spaghetti.

It was a somewhat emotionally difficult task to put mother's spaghetti dish through the ingredient metamorphosis process, but since her mother used ground beef and we do not regularly eat any meat, it had to be changed. We suggest that if you do make it with meat, you make it with ground turkey or free range ground bison (much less chance with bison rather than beef of any unnatural ingredients fed to the animals and passed to you). We have tried it for meat eating family members with both of these and it is excellent tasting.

(The following makes enough for 6 people)

Ingredients for Mother's Saving Grace Spaghetti:

2 cans tomato sauce

1 pound ground beef

1 medium onion, diced small

1 medium green pepper, diced in small pieces

2 stalks of celery, diced in small pieces

½ pound mushrooms, diced in small pieces

2 whole bay leaves

1 tablespoon ground oregano and salt to taste

Steps for Making Saving Grace Spaghetti

1. Cook the ground beef on slow heat so not to burn or make too crispy. Cook until completely done, chop into small pieces and drain off any water.

2. In a large skillet, sauté all the vegetables in vegetable oil. Drain off any excess oil.

3. Add cans of tomato sauce to vegetables. Add spices. Add beef (drained of water).

4. With a lid on top, simmer on low for 30-60 minutes, stirring every 5 minutes. You most likely

will not need to add any water, but if you do just add a few tablespoons.

5. To cook the noodles (mother used regular wheat spaghetti noodles), boil water in a large pot. Be sure and add a tablespoon of oil to the water so the noodles do not stick. Once the water is boiling, add the noodles. Cook about 8 minutes until noodles are tender. You will need to taste test the noodles to make sure they are cooked enough. Or you can just get one noodle out of the boiling pot with your fork and see if you can mush it easily with your fork on a plate. If it is mushy and not still hard, it is cooked.

6. Drain the noodles in a colander. On a plate, add 1 cup noodles. You may wish to take out the bay leaf from the red sauce, although we like to leave it in the left overs to continue seasoning. Then pour (use a ladle if you have one or a big spoon) red sauce all over the top of the spaghetti (about a cup).

7. Top with shredded mozzarella cheese and serve with tossed salad. (To note: Silver Flame only ate the spaghetti as a child, no tossed salad, although her mother always served one.)

Our Altered Healthy Version of Mother's Saving Grace Spaghetti— We Now Call "Secret Ingredient Veggie Spaghetti"

We do love making spaghetti and eating it. We are going to tell you our secret ingredient right away. For many years we have been adding liquid chlorophyll to spaghetti sauce and have never had any of our family members even question why our sauce is a hearty brown color rather than a red. Once you add the green liquid to the red tomato sauce, it turns a brown color, yet does not affect the taste, other than making it seem ever more hearty. The brown gives the appearance of containing meat but ours is vegetarian. We started adding liquid chlorophyll when our children were young in order to get another daily "green" down them (it is made from alfalfa).

Here is one important thing about chlorophyll: it is fairly cheap to buy! And most importantly, it is very healthy for the heart as it is a blood purifier. And it naturally increases the hemoglobin and hematocrit, while at the same time reduces intravascular coagulation without taking blood thinners.

Also, in the late 50s to early 60s, the chief of the US army nutrition branch in Chicago found that high chlorophyll foods reduced the effects of radiation on guinea pigs by 50%. Adding liquid chlorophyll in foods may well be a natural way to add some extra safety from harmful radiation effects in our environment. Now for an amazingly delicious and nutritious spaghetti recipe:

Ingredients:

1 package of organic whole wheat spaghetti noodles, brown rice noodles, or our new favorite organic gluten free Explore Asian Black Bean Spaghetti noodles

organic olive oil (just have the bottle handy)

2 glass jars of organic spaghetti sauce (we avoid cans whenever possible)

1 medium onion, diced small

1 medium green bell pepper, diced small

2 stalks of organic celery, diced small pieces

1 zucchini squash cut in small wedges

½ cup shitake mushrooms, diced in small pieces without any hard stems

2 tablespoon organic dried oregano

2 bay leaves

2 garlic bulb, peeled and diced

3 tablespoons secret ingredient (organic liquid chlorophyll)

a few grinds of black pepper

Steps for Secret Ingredient Spaghetti

1. In a large skill sauté all the vegetables in olive oil. Drain off any excess oil.

3. Add tomato sauce to vegetables. Add spices.

4. With a lid on top, simmer on low for 30 minutes.

5. To cook the noodles, boil water in a large pot. Be sure and add about a tablespoon of oil to the water so the noodles do not stick. Once the water is boiling, add the noodles. Cook about 8 minutes or less if thin noodles (see step #5 on page 56).

6. Drain the noodles in a colander. On a plate, add 1 cup noodles. Then pour (use a ladle if you have one or a big spoon) sauce all over the top of the spaghetti (about a cup or a little more)

7. Top with shredded mozzarella almond cheese and serve with tossed green salad.

The pot is stirred

The contents mixed

And every little thing is fixed.

Your Own Notes and Spells Go Here:

_____

_____

_____

_____

_____

_____

_____

_____

_____

_____

_____

_____

_____

_____

_____

_____

_____

_____

_____

_____

_____

_____

_____

_____

Chapter 4:
Elven Cakes, Breads, and Muffins

Fairy Wing Lemon Cake with Walnut and Lemon Icing Glaze

(Preheat oven to 325 degrees)

Ingredients

Cake Ingredients:

1/2 cup organic extra virgin olive oil*

1 1/2 cup organic white whole wheat flour**

　　or gluten-free flour mix (see page 33)

3 organic omega-3 eggs

1/2 cup organic raw agave or honey

1/2 teaspoon baking powder

　　(organic or Red Mill Brand)

1/2 teaspoon baking soda (non-aluminum)

3/4 cup organic rice milk or almond milk ***

1 tablespoon organic vanilla ****

4 tablespoons organic lemon juice*****

pinch or two of sea salt

8 tablespoons of organic flax meal

1/4 cup chopped walnuts

Icing-Glaze Ingredients:

1 large organic lemon for grated zest

9 tablespoons organic lemon juice

2 tablespoons arrowroot or cornstarch

   (use organic or Red Mill brand)

2 tablespoons of chopped walnuts

Directions

For Baking Cake:

1. Mix eggs and agave, beat, then add lemon juice

2. Add milk, vanilla, and oil to #1

3. Combine flour, salt, baking powder, baking soda, flax meal and add to #2. Mix in walnuts.

4. In lightly oiled and floured large cake pan, bake for 1 hour and 10 minutes (sometimes it takes five or so minutes more) or until a fork that you stick in the middle of cake comes out clean.

For Making Icing:

Pour the lemon juice in a cup, add the arrowroot or cornstarch and stir until dissolved.***** Pour the lemon juice and cornstarch mixture in a little sauce pan, heat over the stove burners (medium to low heat) until the mixture is thickened a little (like a thick gravy consistency). Now add the lemon grated zest (this is optional and only if you have a fresh organic lemon) and also a couple of tablespoons of chopped walnuts.

Once the cake is cooled, take it out of the pan, and pour glaze over the top and spread over entire cake and down sides.

Elf Notes and Tips: For Organic Lemon Cake

* Costco's Kirkland brand has the best deal moneywise on organic extra virgin olive oil

** Organic White Whole Wheat is found at Whole Foods in 5 pound bag King Author Brand

*** We buy our organic rice or almond milk at Costco and by the case. Usually the date is about a year ahead and we have time to use them all up, but we like to always have a case on hand as a survival fall back. Rice milk is not only a good source of protein, but also is a liquid and can be used for drinking if water is scarce. Also remember, in an emergency situation that you can get fresh water, up to 30 to 60 gallons depending on size, from the bottom of your hot water heater. Look for the drain at the bottom of the hot water heater. Just be sure and turn the water heater off first and let the water in it cool down first. If the first couple of gallons have sediment in them, throw that out and take the next gallons. Be sure and boil and treat this water through your water filter. Of course, we hope not to have to use the water from our hot water heaters or from our toilet tanks, so a little preparation is advised. Store a few distilled water bottles in case of outages and shortages in the aftermath of hurricanes and other disturbances in the Force.

**** Simply Organic Vanilla is sold at Safeway and is often on sale. We find it a little cheaper than buying the same brand at health food stores.

***** We always keep a bottle of organic lemon juice on hand, that way you never have to run out of lemon and it is easier than squeezing lemons and picking out all the seeds.

****** Cornstarch will only dissolve in cool liquid so it must be dissolved before it is added to any heated sauces or gravies. Just take a little of the liquid you will be boiling in the recipe and add the cornstarch to it in a separate cup, stir well until it dissolves (which should be easy in this cool state) BEFORE adding it to the boiling pan for heating.

❦

Winter Shaman's Frozen Log Cake: Coconut Milk Whipped Cream with Chocolate

(This cake is made in the freezer, so no preheating!)

Ingredients

12 Double Chocolate Cherry Almond Cookies (see recipe in Cookies Chapter 5, page 94)

1 can (13 oz.) unsweetened organic coconut milk

4 tablespoons organic raw agave or honey

1 tablespoon vanilla

Directions

1. In a freezer tub with lid, place the cookies one by one on top of each other in the tub, stacking them in layers, and lather coconut milk whipped cream* (see Elf Tips for recipe) all over each cookie on both top and sides.

2. Next, when you have the 12 cookies stacked and creamed, turn the whole thing sideways to fit in the container. (You may need fewer cookies to fit the container.) Then add a little remaining cream over the top and sides where there are any places missed. Cover with lid and freeze for 3 hours.

3. When the cake log is completely frozen, take it out of the container and place on a plate. Cut wedges sideways. This is very important. It taste so much better when cut on a diagonal. If you have a little cocoa powder left and/or cinnamon, you can sprinkle a little on top to decorate!

> **Elf Notes & Tips: For Coconut Milk Whip Cream**
>
> *Refrigerate a can of coconut milk overnight. Spoon off the top (water will have settled to the bottom) and whip. If the whipping cream is not all the way stiff, but still like heavy cream, it is still fine. Just use it the best you can and even add extra to the bottom of the container with cookies, freeze for 15 minutes. Take it out and the whipping cream should be a little stiffer and you can spoon the excess on the bottom over the top and between the cookies, then continue freezing. We say this because coconut whipped cream can be hard to stiffen.

Happy Gnomes Banana Nut Bread

(Preheat oven to 375 degrees)

Ingredients

3 or 4 ripe organic bananas (we usually double this recipe and use 7 bananas in all.)

1 tablespoons organic lemon juice (about ½ lemon)

1/3 cup organic olive oil (or a little less)

1/3 cup organic raw agave or honey

1/4 cup organic flaxseed meal (measure after you have ground the seeds into meal)

2 tablespoons ground organic chia seeds (we grind both the flax and chia seeds into meal ourselves using a coffee grinder)

pinch of sea salt

1/2 teaspoon organic or Red Mill brand baking soda

1/2 teaspoon non-aluminum baking powder

1 large or 2 small omega-3 organic eggs

1 and 1/2 cups organic whole wheat or gluten-free flour mix (see page 33)

1 tablespoons organic vanilla (may add a little more if you love vanilla flavor)

2 tablespoon cinnamon

1/3 cup chopped walnuts

1/3 cup organic raisins (optional)

Directions

1. Mash bananas until creamy*

2. Mix lemon juice in with bananas until smooth

3. Cream oil and agave together and then add the banana mixture to it, stirring well.

4. Add eggs to banana-agave mixture and stir well. **

5. In another bowl, add together and sift flour ***, salt, baking powder, and baking soda. Mix together. Add flax meal and chia seed meal and stir well.

6. Add flour mixture to the banana-agave mixture and stir well. Add vanilla and stir.

7. Add nuts and stir. The dough will be a little stiff.

8. Pour into a lightly oiled (olive oil) and floured loaf pan that is 4" by 8" and bake for 50 minutes (or 8" by 8" is okay if you bake for less time—35 minutes for that size). Test to see if done by inserting knife into middle of loaf and if it comes out clean, it is done. Otherwise cook 5 more minutes.

9. Let cool, but while still a little warm, cut into

pieces and put in a refrigerator dish, cover, and refrigerate. ****

Alternative: Try substituting the banana for a cup of fresh mangoes and make Elven Island Mango Nut Bread! It's delicious, particularly if you are lucky enough to get some mangoes grown in Makaha, Oahu!

Elf Notes and Tips: For Banana Nut Bread

* We use a potato masher to mash the bananas so they come out really smashed and creamy.

** When you add the oil and agave, use the same measuring cup. Add the oil first and then the agave. That way, the oil will help the agave slip out of the cup without sticking.

*** You don't have to sift them together. Most people do not sift anymore because flour is pre-sifted. But it can make it an even lighter bread if you do. Most people don't even own a sifter anymore, whereas it used to be in every kitchen.

**** Refrigerating it while it is still warm keeps the condensation in the cookie tin moist. It is fine to wipe the water collected on the inside of the lid off after the first hour of refrigerating.

Peace and Happiness abound,

Ever going round and round.

~

Elfin Island Ginger Bread

(Preheat oven to 350 degrees)

Ingredients

1/2 cup organic olive oil (or a little less since
you are also using flax meal)

1/2 cup organic raw agave or honey (also works
well with ¼ cup honey and 1 teaspoon Stevia)

1 organic omega-3 egg

2 tablespoons Black Strap molasses

1 and ¼ teaspoon baking soda (organic or
Red Mill Brand)

1 & 2/3 cup organic white whole wheat flour*
or gluten-free flour mix (see page 33)

3 tablespoons ground ginger

½ teaspoon clove powder (optional)

1 tablespoon cinnamon**

½ cup boiling drinking water (or use coffee
instead of water for an extra rich flavor)

1 tablespoon organic vanilla

pinch of Himalayan salt ***

5 tablespoons of organic flax meal

1/4 cup chopped walnuts (or use pecans)

1/4 cup organic raisins (optional) ****

Directions

1. We usually double this recipe and use a glass baking dish that is 12" by 8".

2. Mix all dry ingredients except raisins and walnuts (flours and baking soda first, then salt and spices) and then in a separate bowl mix all wet ingredients (except boiling water). Add them together in one bowl. Mix well, and then add hot water to mixture (don't forget the hot water like we did once or you will have a very dry bread).

3. Grease 6" by 10" glass cooking dish with olive oil and lightly flour (dumping excess flour out in trash). We however usually double this recipe and then use an 8" by 14" dish. So, use what you have and double the recipe if it is the longer dish.

4. Pour in batter evenly, and let settle. *****

5. Cook on middle rack for 35 minutes (40 if recipe is doubled. Also. Check to see if done by inserting clean knife in the middle of bread and if the knife comes out clean, it is done. If knife has batter stuck on it, then bake bread 5 more minutes)

6. Let cool, but while still a little warm, cut into pieces and put in a refrigerator dish, cover, and

refrigerate. ******

Elf Notes and Tips: For Elfin Island Ginger Bread

* We have also made this with a substitution of other types of flours. We particularly like using 1/2 cup sorghum flour, 1/2 cup oat flour, and 2/3 cup whole wheat flour. If you double the recipe, try using 2 cups Organic Whole Wheat and 1 ½ cups Organic Buckwheat Flour. Now that is delicious! ** Remember that most cinnamon that you buy in the US is not Ceylon cinnamon, or what is often called "real cinnamon", but is instead Cassia. Cassia cinnamon is a high source of coumarin, a naturally occurring toxin that may potentially damage your liver in high doses. Ceylon contains only traces of coumarin. Ceylon cinnamon may be found in health food stores and we prefer an organic brand—Frontier Organic Fair Trade Ceylon Cinnamon.

*** We have recently learned that Himalayan Salt is the best for you, but you have to be careful from whom you buy it because most companies still use copper sifter/grinders that could have a toxic level of copper left in the salt. So check this out. Find a recommended company that uses a stainless steel grinder.

**** Extra tip: Roll raisins in flour before stirring into bread or cake batters to prevent them from going to bottom.

***** To make sure bubbles are out of the batter,

give the filled dish a little tap on the bottom on your kitchen counter.

****** Refrigerating bread while it is still warm keeps the condensation in the bread tin moist. It is helpful to wipe the water collected on the inside of the lid off after the first hour of refrigerating.

Enchanting Raisin-Walnut Muffins

(Preheat oven to 375 degrees)

Ingredients

2 tablespoons organic olive oil

¾ cup organic rice or almond milk

6 tablespoons organic raw agave

1-2 organic omega-3 eggs (1 okay if large)

2 teaspoon baking powder

¼ teaspoon baking soda

½ cup rolled oats

1 and 1/4 cup organic white whole wheat flour
   or gluten-free flour mix (see page 33)

2 tablespoon cinnamon

1 tablespoon of cloves (optional)

3 tablespoon organic vanilla

pinch of Himalayan salt

9 tablespoons of organic flax meal

1/4 cup chopped walnuts (heart healthy)

1 cup organic raisins

Directions

1. Preheat oven to 375 degrees

2. Mix all dry ingredients (flours and baking soda first, then salt and spices) and then in a separate bowl mix all wet. Add them together in one bowl. Mix well and add raisins and walnuts last.

3. Grease muffin tin with olive oil and lightly flour (dumping excess flour out in trash)

4. Pour in batter filling each cup a little over half full. Should be enough mix for 12 muffins.

5. Cook on middle rack for 18 minutes.

6. Let cool before removing from pan.

Optional topping: Sometimes we like to add dab of a chocolate topping on the top of each muffin. We simply take 3 Tablespoons of Mayan chocolate and mix it with 3 Tablespoons of Raw organic agave. Once it is stirred up together well, it makes a fine chocolate topping, just spoon a teaspoon on top of each muffin and spread.

Adding blueberries: If you substitute blueberries for raisins, be sure and cook the muffins longer, for about 25-30 minutes in all.

Gentle Folk Zucchini Gluten-Free Muffins

(preheat oven at 400 degrees)

Ingredients

> 1/2 cup organic brown rice flour
>
> 1/2 cup sorghum flour
>
> 1/4 cup potato starch
>
> 1/4 cup tapioca starch
>
> 1/3 cup organic raw agave
>
> 1 teaspoon xanthan gum
>
> 2 teaspoon organic cinnamon
>
> 1/2 teaspoon Himalayan salt
>
> 1/2 teaspoon baking powder
>
> 1/2 teaspoon baking soda
>
> 1/3 cup organic olive oil

2 organic large omega-3 free-ranged eggs

1 tablespoons almond milk

2 teaspoon vanilla (or a little more if you are someone who loves vanilla)

1 cup shredded organic zucchini (with peel)

1/2 cup chopped toasted organic almonds

Directions

Toast the nuts whole before adding them to the batter (This brings out their flavor.) Then chop them.

Combine the dry ingredients in a medium mixing bowl.

Add the oil, eggs, milk, and vanilla into the dry mixture. Stir and mix well.

Stir in the zucchini and nuts.

Grease a muffin tin and spoon in batter a little over half way to top

Bake at 400 degrees for 18 minutes.

Heart Healthy Raisin-Walnut Bread

(We make this in a bread maker. If you are baking this all by hand, just be sure and knead well and give rising time before baking. We suggest baking at 375 degrees F.)

Ingredients

(Large Loaf-2 pounds)

1 ½ cups filtered water

3 tablespoons organic extra virgin olive oil

3 teaspoons organic raw agave

1/4 cup organic rice milk or almond milk (or nonfat milk)

3 cups organic white whole wheat flour

1 cup rolled whole oat flour (we grind oats into flour in coffee grinder)

pinch of sea salt

8 tablespoons of organic flax meal (we grind flax and chia seeds in coffee grinder but you can also buy the meal)

4 tablespoons of organic chia seed meal

2 teaspoons active dry yeast (if you make a lot of bread, Costco has a great deal on bread yeast)

Add-in ingredients (add after other ingredients are mixed and first kneading completed):

1 cup organic raisins

3/4 cup chopped walnuts

Directions for Making Bread:

1. Mix all wet ingredients first, then add dry ingredients on top (this is particularly important if you use a bread maker so the yeast does not get wet initially)

2. In convection bread maker, use the large loaf setting for regular bread loaf. If not using bread maker, mix and knead dough according to hand made bread directions below.

3. After first knead, add in the raisins and walnuts.

4. Mix, knead, let rise, and bake. (You may wish to take the bread out of the bread maker before it starts it's last rise and hand knead it a little to make sure all the raisins and nuts are well in the bread)

5. When bread is finished baking, remove and transfer to wire rack to cool.

6. Bread slices best when allowed to cool at least to just slightly warm.

Alternative—Handmade Bread Directions

Turn dough out onto floured board and knead, add small amounts of flour as needed, until the dough is soft and smooth and is not sticky to touch.

Put dough in a lightly olive oiled bowl; turn dough over so that the top of dough is greased. Cover with clean moist kitchen towel and let rise in warm spot for 1 hour (set near window that is sunny or preheated over at 200, but turn oven off before you set it in this time as you are just letting it rise— not cooking the bread).

Next, turn out dough onto floured board and knead.

Now form dough into loaf and set in lightly oiled (use olive oil) bread pan. Cover and let rise for about 30 minutes (not in oven this time).

Preheat oven at 375 degrees F.

Place bread in oven and bake for about 50 minutes or until golden brown.

Turn out bread and let cool on a rack or clean dishtowel. Enjoy!

Now the way will open clear

This food will bring both joy and cheer!

Tip about Bread Makers: We have a Cuisinart

Bread Maker and love it. We have made bread with it nearly every week for 5 years and it is still going strong (knock on wood!). We like that you can cook the bread to the very completion in the bread maker (some bread makers have you bake the last cooking stage in a conventional oven).

Yum-Yum Chocolate Cherry Bread

(preheat oven to 375 degrees) Medium Loaf—1 & 1/2 lbs.

Ingredients

1 cup filtered water

2 tablespoons organic extra virgin olive oil

5 or 6 tablespoons organic raw agave

3 tablespoons organic rice milk or almond milk

2 cups organic white whole wheat flour

1 cup rolled whole oat flour

pinch of sea salt

3 tablespoons of organic flax meal

4 tablespoons raw Mayan organic chocolate

1 & 1/2 heaping teaspoons active dry yeast

Add-in ingredients (add these last two ingredients after other ingredients are mixed and the first kneading is completed):

1/3 cup organic dried cherries (no sugar added)

1/3 cup chopped walnuts

Directions for Making Bread:

This recipe is made in a similar fashion to the recipe for making raisin-walnut bread (see directions of previous recipe). The only difference is in the ingredients and the size is medium rather than large loaf so the bread maker will be set on medium. The baking time will be about 40 minutes or until golden brown. We advise you to play with this recipe and add more cherries to match your own palette. Do be careful not to add too much extra agave as a sweetener because too much sugar in bread will make it hard to rise properly. We usually do not add ground chia seed because they tend to make this recipe too heavy, but you can experiment with it.

Chocolate Chewy Brownies With Healing Beets

(Preheat oven to 325 degrees)

Ingredients

2 cups organic whole wheat flour or gluten-free flour mix (see page 33)

1 cup almond flour (You can substitute pecan meal or even oat flour if you have no almond flour or use organic whole wheat or a wheat substitute if necessary. Try to have almond flour on hand as it will help the protein count of your baked goods.)

6 organic omega-3 free-range eggs

½ cup Mayan Organic Raw Cacao Powder

½ cup organic raw agave or honey (or use ¼ cup honey and 1 teaspoon Stevia)

2 teaspoon baking powder

2 pinches of Himalayan salt

4 tablespoons organic vanilla

1/2 cup organic olive oil

½ cup of beet pulp (saved from juicing)

4 tablespoons of organic flax meal

4 tablespoons of organic chia seeds, finely ground

10 chopped organic almonds for topping

Directions

1. If you have not saved any beet pulp from juicing (remember that it freezes), then make yourself a juice, using the beets first to save the pulp. If you need to use a bit of apple to clear your juicer, a little of its pulp will be fine in this recipe).

2. Mix all dry ingredients first and then add the wet ingredients. We suggest that you add the eggs last in case you want to taste batter for sweetness to your liking (using spoon, of course).

3. Using a glass baking dish about 6 inches by 14 inches, grease it and lightly flour it to get it ready.

4. Pour the batter into the dish. Sprinkle the almonds on top, evenly distributing them.

5. Cook for 50 to 55 minutes in over at 325 degrees. Allow to cool before cutting into squares for brownies.

6. Pour some Mayan Chocolate Syrup from Chapter 7 over brownies.

7. Cut in squares, eat and refrigerate.

It's More than a Scone!
It's an Elf Scone!

(Preheat oven to 400 degrees)

This recipe gives you more than a scone! It is a meal!

Ingredients

1 and ½ cups organic whole wheat flour

1 cup oat flour

1 cup almond flour

6 teaspoons baking powder

2 pinches of Himalayan salt

½ cup organic olive oil

1/3 cup organic raw agave

1 cup almond milk

4 tablespoons organic black strap molasses

2 organic free ranged omega-3 large eggs

4 tablespoons organic finely ground flaxseed

3 tablespoons organic ground chia seeds

3 tablespoons organic cinnamon

2 tablespoons vanilla

½ cup of organic shelled pumpkin seeds

½ cup pine nuts

½ cup organic raisins

½ dried organic cherries

Directions

Lightly grease a cookie sheet.

Combine all dry ingredients in a large bowl—flours, salt, baking powder, flax and chia seeds meal, and cinnamon. Mix oil, milk, vanilla, molasses, agave and eggs together in a separate bowl. Add oil mixture to flour dry mixture until moistened (do not over stir, just until blended). Add fruit and nuts and lightly mix.

Turn dough out onto a lightly floured surface (we use a cutting board) and knead briefly (use plenty of flour on your clean hands). Add more flour if needed to make the dough not sticky.

Using a floured rolling pin (or edge of rounded floured glass), roll out the dough into a ½ inch thick rectangle. Cut with knife squares that are about 2 and ½ inches by 2 and ½ inches.

Place wedges on oiled cookie or baking sheet. Bake for 15 minutes. (stoves are different so check after 12 minutes to see if they are golden brown)

Let cool down before taking off cookie sheet.

The very best

The taste supreme

Will bring to us

Our every dream!

Magic fills this very nook

As every bit of this does cook.

Happiness you'll surely find

As you do taste this dish divine.

Your Own Notes and Spells Go Here:

_____

_____

_____

_____

_____

_____

_____

_____

_____

_____

_____

Chapter 5:
Elf Cookies

Fairy Tale Green Tea Almond Cookies

(Preheat oven to 350 degrees)

Ingredients

- 2 green tea bags* or three tablespoon finely ground green tea
- 1 cup organic white whole wheat flour**
- 1 cup almond flour***
- 2 organic omega-3 egg
- 1/2 cup organic raw agave
- 1 teaspoon baking powder (organic or Red Mill Brand non-aluminum)
- 1 tablespoon organic vanilla
- 1/2 cup organic olive oil (or a little less since you are also using flax meal)
- 1 teaspoon organic almond extract****
- pinch or two of Himalayan sea salt

6 tablespoons of organic flax meal

about 8 chopped almonds for top of cookies

Directions

1. Preheat oven to 350 degrees

2. Mix all dry ingredients and then in a separate bowl mix all wet ingredients. Add them together in one bowl.

3. On lightly oiled cookie sheet, spoon drops of cookie dough (about 2 tablespoons per cookie or a little less). Press each cookie with large spoon and flatten on pan.

4. Place a couple of small pieces of almond on top of each cookie and flatten into cookie a little with spoon.

5. Cook on highest rack (so bottoms do not burn) for about

12 to 15 minutes. *****

For an alternative, we sometimes add about 1/3 cup of cooked and mashed purple Okinawan sweet potatoes. It is delicious and adds important nutrition to the recipe. You can even change it up more and have a completely different cookie if you eliminate the green tea and add as much as ½ cup of the sweet potato.

When we do that we also add an extra tablespoon vanilla.

Elf Notes and Tips: For Green Tea Cookies

* Stash Green Tea powder or some similar powder form of green tea (best from Japan).

** If you double the recipe, you can substitute oatmeal for one cup of the flour or almond meal.

*** We use the Organic King Author Brand found at Whole Foods and Down to Earth.

**** We use Frontier brand.

*****For softer cookies, only cook 12-13 minutes.

Windwalkers' Oatmeal Raisin Cookies

(Preheat oven to 350 degrees)

Ingredients

1 cup rolled oats (Red Mill brand or organic)

1 cup organic whole wheat flour * or

gluten-free flour mix (see page 33)

1 cup almond or quinoa flour

2 organic omega-3 egg

1/2 cup organic raw agave

4 tablespoons black strap molasses

1/2 teaspoon baking powder (organic or

Red Mill Brand non-aluminum)

1/2 teaspoon baking soda

2 or 3 tablespoons organic vanilla **

2 tablespoons cinnamon

1/2 cup organic olive oil (or a little less since

you are also using flax meal)

pinch of Himalayan salt

4 tablespoons of organic flax meal or Red

Mill Brand ***

1/2 cup organic raisins (add a little more if

you like, we do sometimes.)

1/4 cup chopped walnuts

Directions

1. Mix all dry ingredients and then in a separate bowl mix all wet ingredients. Add them together in one bowl.

2. On lightly oiled cookie sheet, drop one-inch balls of dough (about 2 tablespoons per cookie or a little less). Press each cookie with large spoon and flatten on pan.

3. Cook on highest rack (so bottoms do not burn) for about 12 to 15 minutes.

Elf Notes and Tips: For Oatmeal Raisin Cookies

* Here is a tip for all your flours and grains like rice, corn meal, etc: When you first buy it, put it in the freezer for 48 hours, then you can move it to your regular grain storage area. This amount of freezing will kill any microscopic maggot eggs, mealworms and other larval forms, etc. We always do this and even store flours in the freezer for longer periods if there is room, just to fill the space. (remember: a full refrigerator cuts down on electricity and this is true of your freezer as well). Of course, it goes without saying that if you see any wiggly or dormant worms in your grains then toss it all out!

** If you can find fresh vanilla beans, split them down lengthwise and scrape out the inner substance. This makes the best vanilla flavoring!

*** If you can only find flax seeds, grind them finely in your coffee bean grinder. You can use your coffee bean grinder to grind nuts and seeds like Chia to add in recipes for flavor and nutrition.

☙

Mystic Oatmeal Cranberry Cookies

(Preheat oven to 350 degrees)

You may also try this recipe using dried organic cherries. Cranberries may be easier to find in the winter and cherries in the spring and summer. When we use dried cherries, we use just a little less agave because the cherries have a natural sweetness. Don't be afraid to use your tasting spoons to adjust the amount to your palette. If you use dried cherries, they do not need to be cooked like the cranberries.

Ingredients

1 cup rolled oats (Red Mill brand or organic)

1 cup organic whole wheat flour or

gluten-free flour mix (see page 33)

1 cup almond or quinoa flour

2 organic omega-3 egg

1/2 cup organic raw agave

1/2 teaspoon non-aluminum baking powder

1/2 teaspoon baking soda

2 tablespoons organic vanilla

2 tablespoons cinnamon

1/2 cup organic olive oil (or a little less since

you are also using flax meal)

pinch of Himalayan salt

4 tablespoons of organic flax meal

1/4 cup chopped walnuts

1 cup whole cooked cranberries (see following
directions)

Cooking the cranberries before adding them to the cookie dough

Place 10 oz. of cranberries in a boiler (we use organic frozen ones). Add 1/3 cup water and a couple of tablespoons of agave. Let come to a boil and cook for 2 minutes, just as berries begin to pop open. Try not to overcook them, as you want them to be whole and not mushy. Let cool, stir, and strain out the liquid into a cup or small bowl. The berries are now ready to add to the mix, but remember that you add them at the very last. This way they only get tossed lightly into the cookie dough mix and don't turn too mushy. And, by the way, you can use the liquid you poured off the berries as a base for some delicious cranberry lemonade, just have to add about four cups of water and a little more agave to taste.

Directions

1. Mix all dry ingredients and then in a separate bowl mix all wet ingredients, except the cranberries. Add dry and liquid ingredients together in one bowl

and stir well. Now add the cranberries last after everything is well stirred and toss them in lightly just so they are part of the mix.

2. On lightly oiled cookie sheet, drop one-inch balls of dough (about 2 tablespoons per cookie or a little less). Press each cookie with large spoon and flatten lightly on pan.

3. Cook on highest rack (so bottoms do not burn) for about 20 minutes. (These cookies have extra water in them from the cranberries, so they cook longer than most cookies. If you use dried cranberries, you would only cook them for 12-15 minutes).

Nether Realms Double Chocolate Cherry Cookies

(Preheat oven to 350 degrees)

These delicious cookies are heart healthy cookies, in that not only is the dark chocolate, olive oil, and the flaxseed meal heart healthy ingredients, but also the flour used is half organic whole wheat and half almond flour, which makes it 1 to 1 on the carbohydrate to protein ratio. This recipe makes about 2 dozen cookies. We suggest doubling all ingredients in it to make 4 dozen because these cookies freeze really well in small batches in the refrigerator, so you can spread eating them out over a few weeks.

Ingredients

1/2 cup organic whole wheat flour or

gluten-free flour mix (see page 33)

1/2 cup almond flour

3 medium organic omega-3 eggs

1/3 heaping cup Mayan Organic Raw Cacao

Powder

1/3 cup organic raw agave

1 teaspoon baking soda

1 tablespoon organic vanilla

1/3 cup organic olive oil

3 tablespoons of organic flax meal

1/4 cup dried organic cherries (no added

sweeter)

2 tablespoons finely ground chia seeds

10 chopped organic almonds for topping

Directions

1. Mix all dry ingredients first and then add the wet ingredients. We suggest that you add the eggs last in case you want to taste batter for adding any extra

agave for sweetness to your liking (using spoon of course).

2. On well-oiled cookie sheet, drop about 1 heaping tablespoons per cookie. If you need to use your hands, slightly wet them so the batter does not stick to your hands. Sprinkle a few chopped pieces of almonds on top of each cookie and then press them with large spoon and flatten lightly on pan.

3. Cook on highest rack (so bottoms do not burn) for about 12-13 minutes. These cookies will harden slightly after they come out of the oven, so do not overcook them. Enjoy!

Faerie Magic come to be

With every bite it doth fill me (thee).

Your Own Notes and Spells Go Here:

_____

_____

_____

_____

_____

_____

Chapter 6:
Faerie Pies

Basic Altered Healthy Pie Crust

The Basic Altered Healthy Pie Crust is the pie crust we use for all pies requiring a crust. We created it by altering Silver Flame's mother's basic pie crust recipe that is listed below:

2 cups flour (she meant white flour)

¼ teaspoon salt

2/3 cup butter (keep in freezer until right

before using) or vegetable oil

4 to 5 tablespoons cold water

Directions: Combine flour and salt, cut in butter, stir in cold water.

Basic Altered Healthy Pie Crust Ingredients

1 cups organic whole wheat flour or gluten-

free flour mix (see page 33) or substitute

other baking flours, see Chapter 1

1/2 cup almond flour (or substitute whole
wheat or other gluten-free flour mix
substitutes if you do not have nut flours)

1/4 cup organic flax meal

1/3 cup olive oil

2 shakes of Himalayan salt

2 Tablespoons organic raw agave (optional
but our family loves a little sweetening
added)

1 egg (optional if you are allergic, but can
help bind the dough)

1/4 cup cold water

Directions for Making the Pie Dough

The first step in making any pie is to make the
pie dough. Combine the dry ingredients, then add wet
ingredients, and last add cold water, stir best you can
then knead with your very clean hands. First flour
your hands so the wet ingredients do not stick to
them. Do not stir or knead any more than necessary to
mix it well. Roll out with floured rolling pin (or use a
tall glass if you do not have a rolling pin) on a floured
cutting board or flat surface. You will need to roll it

out in all four directions to make it wide enough to lie in the pie dish. Then carefully place it in the pie shell (fold it in half to move it if you have to and then spread it back out once in the pie dish). Use a knife to cut off the excess dough around the very top of the sides. Now your dough is ready to cook. Until time to use it, put it to the side rolled in a ball with a wet clean cloth on top.

Pixie Pumpkin/Sweet Potato Pie with Rice Milk

(Preheat oven to 425 degrees)

Pie Filling Ingredients

16 ounces can pumpkin (we used a 15-ounce can of organic pumpkin) or well mashed sweet potatoes

2/3 cup organic raw agave

1 tablespoon ground cinnamon

1 teaspoon ground ginger

1/2 teaspoon ground nutmeg (and we did look it up, and nutmeg is not a nut)

pinch of salt

1 and 1/2 cup rice milk that has been

thickened with powdered non-fat dry milk

(start with 1 and $1/4^{th}$ cup of rice milk and add

1 cup powdered organic dry milk to thicken

it. Mix well and use only 1 and ½ cups for

recipe)

3 slightly beaten eggs

2 tablespoons organic whole wheat flour

Directions for Making Pie

1. Roll out the pie dough (use standard pie crust recipe at beginning of this chapter) for the crust and place into a pie dish. Put into oven to bake for 5 minutes or so, just to brown the crust. This crust will only be somewhat pre-cooked, where as other pies like the next recipe—chocolate pie— will not be baked after the pie filling is in it and so it will be pre-baked longer to be completely cooked.

2. Combine pumpkin (or sweet potato), agave, cinnamon, ginger, nutmeg, and salt. Add eggs. Beat until just combined. Add the 2 tablespoons flour to the rice milk and stir well. Now gradually stir in rice milk to the rest of the mixture.

3. Pour filling into pre-cooked piecrust.

4. Cover just the edges of the pie crust with tin foil, in order to keep them from over-browning and leave the foil on until the last 15 minutes of baking time. Bake in 425-degree oven for the first 15 minutes. Reduce the temperature to 350 degrees and bake another 30 minutes (or until a knife inserted near the center comes out clean)

5. Let it cool down and then refrigerate for at least 2 hours before serving. Serves 6 to 8.

6. If you taste a little of the pie filling from the edge of the pie and it is not spicy enough, then you can always sprinkle more spices on top.

This was the tastiest low dairy pumpkin pie that we've managed to make, and we'll definitely be cooking more of these! (Many other pumpkin pie recipes we tried creating and tested had filling that was just too runny. This one is perfect!)

Mages' Mayan Chocolate Cream Pie

(Preheat oven to 375 degrees)

Have one prebaked single crust pie shell ready (see pie crust recipe at beginning of this chapter and bake the crust for 20 minutes so it is completely cooked).

Ingredients

Pie Ingredients:

8 Tablespoons organic Mayan dark chocolate powder, unsweetened*

1/2 cup organic raw agave

9 tablespoons organic cornstarch

3 cups organic almond or rice milk

1 cup thickened powdered organic non-fat milk or use no dairy and just add almond milk and it simply requires more cornstarch to thicken (thicken to the consistency of kefir) **

1 teaspoon organic vanilla

pinch or two of sea salt

Directions for Making Pie

In double boiler, mix agave, cocoa powder, cornstarch mixture***, and salt.

1. Add almond milk and mix together.

2. Place double boiler over boiling water and cook about 5 to 10 minutes stirring constantly. Reduce heat to low when it thickens. **** You only need to cook it about 2 minutes on low heat after it thickens.

3. Remove from heat and allow to cool slightly, and then add vanilla while stirring.

4. Pour into prebaked pie shell. Cool in refrigerator at least 2 hours before serving.***** Optional: Top each piece with coconut whipped cream (see page 66)!

Elf Notes and Tips:

* We use Organic Raw Chocolate Powder, Mayan Superfood from health food stores. If you use chocolate bitter squares then 2 tablespoons = 1 square, so you need three melted. In a double boiler so it does not burn.

** We buy Organic Valley's nonfat dry milk from a health food store.

*** Be sure and stir cornstarch in a little cool liquid, as it will not dissolve in hot liquid. We usually use about ¼ of the almond or rice milk to mix it in and then pour it in to boiler.

****We have used a regular boiling pan and it works fine, but you have to watch it closely and stir the entire time it cooks. Also, once it boils, turn the heat down to medium low so it boils slowly and does not burn.

***** A word about freezing this pie for later. We did it and it worked fine but it needs to unfreeze in the refrigerator.

Faerie Island Apple Pie #1

(Preheat oven to 350 degrees)

Ingredients

6 organic apples (if Gaia then may need extra agave)

½ cup organic raw agave (little less is apples are sweet)

2 pinches Himalayan salt

1 and ½ tablespoons organic cornstarch or organic arrowroot

½ teaspoon organic cinnamon

¼ teaspoon nutmeg (fresh grated if possible)

2 or 3 tablespoons organic lemon juice

¼ teaspoon clove powder (optional)

3 tablespoons organic vanilla

small amount of organic almond or rice milk

Directions

1. Peel, core, thinly slice the apples

2. Combine cornstarch, salt, and spices. Sprinkle over apples and toss.

3. Sprinkle lemon juice, agave, and vanilla on apples and toss lightly until evenly blended.

4. Divide dough from recipe at the beginning of this chapter into two parts. Roll out one part into a pie crust. Place apples in rolled out bottom crust shell (uncooked). Then roll out rest of dough and cut strips. Place the dough strips on top of the pie in a crisscross.

5. Wet rim of pie crust with almond milk so it does not burn while cooking

6. Bake 40 minutes. Cool before cutting to eat.

Faerie Island Apple Pie #2

(preheat over 350 degrees)

This is another version of Faerie Island Apple Pie #1 except that it uses more juice and is for those who like their pies a little wet.

Directions

1. Using same ingredients as Faerie Island Apple Pie #1, cook cut apple slices in boiling water for about 4 minutes (use spoon to test softness).

2. Next, in separate cup or glass, add ¼ cup fresh squeezed orange juice or pomegranate juice (this is the only different ingredient from Faerie Island Apple

Pie#1) with 2 tablespoons arrowroot (this is a little more than Pie#1). Stir and mix well. Always mix arrowroot or cornstarch in cool liquid before adding to any other mixture (it will not dissolve well and lumps up in hot liquids). If you use pomegranate juice then you may need a little more agave; and a little less agave than the ½ cup may be possible if you use orange juice (depending on the sweetness of the apples).

3. Add salt and spices, lemon juice, agave and vanilla to the apple mixture and stir.

4. Divide dough from recipe at the beginning of this chapter into two parts. Roll out one part into a pie crust. Place apples in rolled out bottom crust shell (uncooked). Then roll out rest of dough and place the second dough sheet on top of the pie. Cut with knife around the edges so the pie crust top fits like a lid. Next go around the pie crust edges with a fork and press. Carefully poke little slits in the top crust with knife.

5. Wet rim of pie crust with almond milk so it does not burn while cooking

6. Bake 40 minutes. Cool before cutting to eat.

☙

Magically Delicious Healthy Cherry Pie

(Preheat oven to 375 degrees)

This is our favorite cherry pie! These elves love cherry pie. This recipe is adopted from Silver Flame's mother's family cherry pie recipe using some organic ingredient substitutions, including raw agave instead of sugar. You can try substituting other berries. Raspberries work particularly well as a substitution for the cherries.

Ingredients

4 cups organic cherries (we use organic cherries in the can—but you can buy, wash, deseed, and boil for 5 minutes in ½ cup filtered water on stove top 4 cups of fresh cherries). It usually takes 2 cans of cherries.

1 cup organic raw agave

dash of Himalayan salt

¼ cup cherry juice (saved from drained can of cherries or from boiled cherries)

¼ teaspoon fresh lemon juice

3 tablespoons organic cornstarch

1 teaspoon organic cinnamon

Optional: ¼ teaspoon ground cloves

Directions

Mix cornstarch and salt. Add ¼ cup cherry juice (let cool down first if from boiled cherries) and make a paste.

In saucepan, mix 1 cup agave and remaining ½ cup cherry juice and bring to a boil.

Then slowly add the cornstarch paste mixture. Stir until blended.

Add cherries, spices, and lemon juice. Let cook a minute or 2 until mixture is thickened.

Using the pie crust recipe from the beginning of this chapter, pour cherry mixture into shell. Make a crisscross pie crust top (using strips of dough).

To make sure the crust does not burn, you may wish to brush some almond milk on the rim of the crust to wet it and/or bake the pie with tin foil pieces around the rim up after the first 15 minutes of baking.

Bake on 375 degrees for 1 hour.

Ingredients I stir and bind

With happiness that each will find.

Silver Elves Favorite Twilight Dessert—Mango Ice cream

Place 1 and 1/2 cup of frozen organic mango pieces (Costco sells them in their frozen fruit section) in a blender. Pour enough Mango Naked Juice (other juice like orange is not thick enough to work so must be Mango) over the mango pieces to cover an inch or two above them in the blender. Add ½ cup of Greek yogurt or for non-dairy use 1/3 cup coconut whipped cream (See Elf Tips, page 66). Blend completely. Pour into a freezer container with lid. Put in freezer. After about 2 hours, should be set enough to eat. If you leave it overnight, just let it stand out of the freezer on your kitchen counter for about 45 minutes until it softens a little. You want to eat it when it is fairly easy to spoon out but not yet back to liquid. It takes a bit of practice to get the thawing timing just right. It is fine to keep refreezing what is left over and thawing it to serve (lasts for several days).

Papayas will also work for this recipe and make a good after dinner treat for digestion. Although mangoes have a healthy alkaline level, we also like to use cherries. The cherry blend makes a delicious substitution for milk with your granola and we often like to replicate an acai bowl with it. Also, you may try soaking Chia seeds in rice milk, refrigerating them an hour, blending them well, and then topping them with this fruit mixture).

We Silver Elves eat this almost every twilight to enhance sweet dreams with no dessert weight gain the next morning.

Friends forever we shall be

As you do taste with ecstasy.

Your Own Notes and Spells Go Here:

_____

_____

_____

_____

_____

_____

_____

_____

_____

_____

_____

_____

_____

_____

_____

_____

_____

_____

Chapter 7:
Main Entrées with Some Side Dishes

Goddess Cauliflower and Potato

This is a recipe we first learned from our friend Menuka, the Nepalese Goddess of Chia Tea, and have altered it somewhat to be vegetarian. The original dish also has chicken pieces in it, which you are welcome to add.

Ingredients

2 large or 4 small organic red potatoes cut into small pieces

1 small cauliflower cut in small pieces

1 small onion cut in slices

2 garlic cloves, peeled and cut in small pieces

¼ teaspoon cumin

½ teaspoon chili power

¼ teaspoon turmeric

2 shakes Himalayan salt

¼ fenugreek seeds

1 teaspoon fresh ginger pieces

1 large organic local tomato, chopped

¼ cup cilantro, chopped

organic olive oil (have bottle handy)

Directions

1. Pour about 1 tablespoons oil in large frying pan. Heat pan to low heat. Fry fenugreek seeds in oil.

2. Add about 2 more tablespoons oil and brown onion in oil with fenugreek seeds. Let the onions cook slow and as long as it takes for them to be caramelized (richly brown).

3. Next add another tablespoon of oil and the cauliflower, potatoes and turmeric. Toss and let it cook for 8 minutes, stirring every 2 minutes.

4. About 4 minutes into the cooking process, add the garlic, cumin, chili powder, and salt and stir.

5. Add the tomatoes and cilantro after cooked. Toss and serve over brown rice or to side. (We prefer to cook our brown rice with saffron and eat as yellow saffron rice. Just add large pinch of saffron at the beginning to the water and rice in your rice cooker and it will come out as delicious yellow saffron rice)

6. Goes well with mint sauce (see chapter 9).

7. Serve with chia tea in your chalice.

Ancient Elves' One Dish, Easy Baked Veggies and Fish (optional)

An easy-to-make and nutritious meal for the non-cooks in the family and for ancient elves who cannot stand long on their feet in the kitchen, but would like to still enjoy cooking some home cooked meals. With just this one recipe, one can enjoy cooking for oneself and others well into old age!

(Preheat oven to 250 degrees)

This recipe is for all you who don't generally cook, but find yourself in a position where people are expecting a meal from you. It is also for anyone who feels particularly unable to do much in the kitchen one night but would like an amazing hot dinner.

Ingredients

3 tablespoons organic olive oil

2 medium Irish and 2 sweet potatoes (try purple Okinawan)

2 medium carrots

1 medium onion

½ pound whole mushrooms

1 medium red bell pepper

1 medium whole tomatoes

1 large beet

cup of Brussels sprouts

8 oz. green string beans

½ cup cauliflower rosettes

½ cup zucchini (or other squash)

½ cup of organic small carrots

Steps for Making Baked Vegetables

1. Preheat oven to 250 degrees

2. Wash well, cut off stems and then slice all veggies in approximately one inch size pieces (like you were going to stir fry them). Dry them all by blotting with a paper towel. Many veggies will oven roast but avoid leafy greens like kale, spinach, lettuce, and collards due to the high water content.

3. Pour all the vegetables in a large mixing bowl and add 3 tablespoons organic olive oil. Season it with garlic powder, a few pinches of Himalayan salt, and your favorite spice for vegetables. We like to sprinkle curry powder on ours but sometimes we use

rosemary instead. Your choice!

4. After oiling and seasoning your vegetables, lay them out on a flat baking sheet in a single layer. If you want a very easy cleaning job, place a piece of parchment paper down on the baking sheet for the veggies to cook on.

5. Most vegetables will roast in about 15-22 minutes. Vegetables like onions and peppers can be roasted in as little as 8 minutes, whereas potatoes and carrots may take the full 22 minutes. During roasting, turn over the vegetables once or twice to keep them from sticking or burning.

6. Once you have roasted all your vegetables, place them in a large serving bowl for the dinning table. If you also roast a fish, use the same procedure but a different pan to separate the taste. We suggest that you cook your fish with pineapple slices along side and serve that up on a platter on the table with the vegetables, add a green salad and some bread, then you will have quite a feast for yourself and guests. If your guests are vegetarians, serve veggies as a standalone meal or with frying pan sautéed garden burgers and a sauce (like mustard sauce) rather than fish. You may wish to make a tarter sauce (see chapter 9) for your fish. Roasted vegetables also save and reheat in the microwave the next day or two.

Rainbow Oven Baked Fruit

Do you ever have quite a bit of fruit that is ripe and needs to be eaten soon? We once had a neighbor in Makaha give us more ripe papayas from their tree than we could eat. Since we had always loved baked pineapples with fish, we decided to try baking the papayas too. We prepared them the same as baked veggies in the previous recipe and baked the papayas for just 15 minutes at 250 degrees. Baking the fruit brought out the flavor and honestly tasted even better than fresh. Since that time, we have also tried baking a rainbow of fruits including: pears, mangoes, peaches, plums and apples. We don't even feel they need agave added, but you could if you have a sweet tooth. You may need to reconstitute some fruit once it is oven baked by sprinkling a small amount of orange juice or mango juice evenly on top. Serve fruit warm.

Meal in a Pumpkin—A Genii's Delight

This was something Silver Flame's mother made up and would serve her and her sister Gail as children. Using the inside of a small pumpkin she had carved the pulp out of (for pie) and then cleaned the inside, she would serve them left-overs in a bowl set down in the pumpkin. What a magic surprise!

Wyzards' Roman Hawaiian Pizza

(For a Large pizza: Preheat oven to 500 degrees)

Ingredients for Dough

1 cup plus 3 tablespoons purified water

¾ teaspoon raw organic agave

2 pinches of Himalayan salt

1 ½ tablespoons organic virgin olive oil

4 tablespoons finely ground organic flaxseeds

3 ¼ cups organic whole wheat flour or

gluten-free flour mix (see page 33)

1 ¾ teaspoons of active dry yeast

Ingredients for Toppings

8 oz. of almond mozzarella style cheese, no
GMO (or use cows milk mozzarella if you
like, as in Rome, and especially healthy for
your gut is a raw milk cheese like
Parmigiano Reggiano)

1 8 oz. jar of organic tomato pizza sauce

1 cup of sliced shitake mushrooms

½ cup Chinese eggplant sliced in thin silver
dollar size

½ cup sliced onions

½ cup sliced organic red bell peppers

¼ cup sliced pieces of fresh pineapple

3-5 Tablespoons organic extra virgin olive oil

1 Tablespoon ground organic oregano

2 pinches of Himalayan salt

black pepper

garlic powder (optional)

(Other toppings are up to you. Other suggested toppings are fresh sliced zucchini, garlic pieces, sliced black olives, diced tomatoes. Be sure and sauté all veggies in olive oil before using as a topping.)

Directions

For the Dough: We make this in our bread maker, however we do on occasions make it by hand, as it is so easy to do. Mix using a wooden spoon the ingredients in a large bowl. Place dough on a lightly floured surface (we use a large cutting board) and knead in a small amount of extra flour to make the dough a little stiff, but remaining stretchy—elastic. Now place a damp kitchen towel over the dough for about half an hour giving it a little rising time.

Note: Prepare the toppings (see instructions next

page) while the dough sits to rise. You always want to have your toppings ready for the assembling of the pizza as soon as you have the dough rolled out. If the dough sits around after being rolled out and placed on the pizza pan, it is going to be easier for it to stick to the pan when you cook it.

Once the dough has sat to rise a half of an hour: On a floured surface, roll out the dough in a circle. Use a rolling pin (flour it lightly) if you have one, otherwise, use a tall drinking glass (flour it lightly) turned sideways as a makeshift rolling pin. Roll out the dough to a little larger than the circle size of your pizza pan. Carefully fold the dough in half (makes it easier to carry and transport to pan without it breaking) and then half again. Place dough on your lightly floured pizza pan (use some organic whole wheat flour or organic corn meal) and situate the dough as a round, then build up the sides by pinching around the edges to make it perfectly fitting. This will help hold the sauce without spilling out in the toppings steps ahead. Some people cook the dough about 5 minutes on 350 at this point (and then 6 minutes more later after the toppings are on it at 500 degrees). We usually do not cook it until after we have placed the sauce, cheese and all the toppings on and then we cook the pizza 10 minutes at 500 degrees.

For the Toppings:

In a frying pan, use half of the olive oil (just have the bottle handy if it looks like you may need to add more to keep veggies from sticking to pan) and lightly sauté the peppers first (add a pinch of salt while cooking), then the mushrooms (add the oregano and the other pinch of salt while you sauté the mushrooms), then sauté the onions. Last, using the remaining olive oil (or add a little more as egg plant is dry), sauté the sliced eggplant pieces. Place each cooked topping in separate small bowls or divide on a large plate. Grate the cheese in separate bowl or go Roman style and slice pieces ¼ inch (not too thick so it melts easily).

Assembling the Pizza:

Now evenly spread the pizza tomato sauce all over the dough. (If you do not have pizza sauce and would like to make your own, then use one can tomato sauce and one can tomato paste. Mix together and add some oregano and pinch of salt. Add a little water if too thick. Remember that pizza sauce has the consistency of a thick ketchup.) You can sprinkle a little more oregano on the sauce once it is spread out and also if you like garlic, you may sprinkle some garlic powder. Next add your cheese evenly over the pizza. And then add each topping one by one, adding the pineapple last. We noticed while spending some time in Rome that Italian pizza is generally made with each topping clustered separately on top rather than spreading toppings evenly all over the pizza American style. And yes, Hawaiian pizza was on the menu in Rome! Personally, we like toppings evenly spread, but you may wish to try it Roman style. You may also like to add a small amount of ground black pepper on top.

In a preheated oven to 500 degrees, bake for 10 minutes. Ovens vary in temperature so you may need a little longer or shorter. Be sure and let it cool a little before slicing and eating.

Elves' Squash Dish

We once had a squash garden in Sonoma County, Ca. that grew enormous squash of all sorts. It was a volunteer garden that stretched across our entire back and part of our side yard. We just threw out all our squash seeds randomly into the garden area and let the nature spirits do all the work from there. We particularly loved the Carnival Squash, but honestly there were so many varieties of squash popping up all the time that we mixed and matched them in our recipes and were never disappointed in the delightful flavors they rendered.

(preheat oven at 325 degrees)

Ingredients

2 large squash or four small (Delicata, Carnival, Buttercup, Banana or Autumn Cup, etc.)

1 medium-small onion

1 cup medium sharp non-GMO cheese, goat or almond cheese

¼ teaspoon ground ginger (or finely grated fresh)

¼ teaspoon oregano or sage

a couple of pinches of Himalayan salt and pepper

½ cup chopped walnuts

Directions

Wash the squash, peel and dice. Place the squash and nuts in a large oven baking pan.

Sauté the onion in olive oil and then stir into squash.

Add seasoning and toss. Add a small amount of

filtered water to the mixture (like 4 tablespoons). Bake at 325 degrees for about 30 minutes or until the squash is tender. Then add cheese on top and return to the oven, this time with the lid on it. Cook another 10 minutes until cheese is melted.

If you have some breadcrumbs, they go well sprinkled on top of each serving or use a couple of tablespoons of ground flaxseed meal. Serve with a piece of homemade bread, organic corn on the cob, and a tossed green salad (organic spinach) with avocado & sprouts and you have a great vegetarian meal.

෴

Gypsies' Elfin Potato and Mushroom Delight

(Preheat oven to 325 degrees)

Silver Flame created this dish in her 20s and have been making it ever since. It can be used as a main entrée or side dish. People love it! We once took this dish to a potluck at Oberon and Morning Glory Zell Ravenheart's house. Every one else had brought store bought desserts. The Pagans went wild over this dish and there was not a scrap left. We almost didn't have to wash the casserole pan.

Ingredients

8 large potatoes

1 medium onion, chopped

1 pound mushrooms (We always like to use shitake mushrooms for their nutrient content and alkaline level, but any of your favorite type will work fine in this recipe.)

16 oz organic low-fat Greek yogurt or Nancy's Organic Probiotic low-fat yogurt

1 teaspoon Himalayan salt

a few grinds of fresh pepper

16 oz of medium sharp cheese, raw milk goat cheese, or almond cheese

4 tablespoons of pine nuts

also have a bottle of organic olive oil handy

Directions

Wash and peel the potatoes (we like to leave as much of the peel on the potatoes as possible if they are organic and the peel is not tough), then cut in slices and boil about 10 minutes or until tender (stick a fork in potato to see if it is mushy, if not, keep boiling). Drain the potatoes and mash. Add a few tablespoons almond milk and whip until you have beautiful mashed potatoes. Add the salt and pepper.

While the potatoes are boiling, wash and cut the mushrooms and onions in small pieces. Sauté them separately in a little olive oil on the stovetop. Put then in separate bowls to use for your casserole later.

Grate your cheese and put in a separate bowl to use later.

Using a large casserole dish, oil the bottom slightly with olive oil. Now put down a layer of potatoes about an inch thick, next a layer of yogurt about ½ inch thick, next a layer of onions (just enough to cover), next a layer of mushrooms (about ¼ inch thick), and last a layer of the cheese. Continue layering until all your ingredients are gone (usually about 3-4 layers of each). You should end up with cheese on top.

If your family likes garlic, you may add fresh garlic to the sautéed veggies or sprinkle garlic power with onions. Also, you may need to salt to your own taste as we use very little salt. But potatoes are a food that needs salt for the flavor to come out.

Now place the casserole in the oven and bake covered for 30 minutes.

After the casserole is cooked and the cheese is completely melted, sprinkle pine nuts evenly on top (sliced almonds are also good if you are out of pine nuts).

Optional: we often also add a layer of chopped pieces of about 4-6 veggie or bean burgers of various types (try adding some of the falafels or navy bean burgers in the following 2 recipes). Originally, in the 70s, Silver Flame made it with a layer of ground meat and you are welcome to do the same if you feel you need the extra protein.

Falafels Elfin

These are a great source of protein for people who have cut meat out of their diets. It's fairly low in fat and has no cholesterol if you fry it in heart-healthy oil (grape seed). Falafels were originally made in Egypt and other Arab countries using fava beans. However, the Israeli falafel is made from chickpeas (otherwise known as garbanzo beans) flour. Often Jewish people have a hereditary enzymatic deficiency (G6PD) that can be triggered by fava beans, so chickpeas are used instead in their meals. If you have no such medical condition then by all means try both beans out and experiment with which is the best for you. If you make it Egyptian style with fava beans, also leave out the cilantro.

Ingredients

1 cup dried chickpeas (or one can)

1 medium onion, chopped

2 tablespoons finely chopped organic parsley

2 tablespoons finely chopped organic cilantro

1 teaspoon Himalayan salt

2 cloves of garlic

1 large omega-3 egg

2 tablespoons fresh lemon juice

3 tablespoons of ground flax seed meal

1 teaspoon cumin

1 teaspoon baking powder

4-6 tablespoons organic whole wheat flour

organic grape seed oil bottle handy (or olive oil if you do not have grape)

Chopped organic tomato pieces (as garnish)

Diced onion (as garnish)

Diced red organic bell pepper (as garnish)

Tahini sauce

Pita bread

Directions

1. Soak chickpeas overnight in filtered water (cover 3 inches above peas). Drain. You may also use canned chickpeas.

2. Place the chickpeas, onions, parsley, cilantro, salt, garlic, egg, lemon juice, and cumin in a food processor (blender will also work). Process until blended (not pureed).

3. Add the baking powder, 4 tablespoons of flour and flaxseed meal. Blend. Add enough extra flour so that the dough forms a small ball and no longer sticks to your hands. Put mixture in a bowl, cover and refrigerate for 3-4 hours.

4. When refrigerated, form the chickpea mixture into balls about the size of a silver dollar, but round.

5. Fry in olive oil. First try 1 ball to test. If it falls apart, add a little more flour. Then fry about 6-8 balls at once for about 3 minutes on each side, or until golden brown. Drain on paper towels. You may eat the falafels separately on a plate or stuff half a pita round with falafel balls, along with chopped tomatoes, onion, and red bell pepper. (We also like grated cucumber.)

6. Sprinkle tahini sauce on top.

❧

Mermaid Navy Bean—Pine Nut Burgers

Makes a moderately alkaline food, with a protein-carbohydrate balance, and dense nutritional ingredients.

Ingredients

1/3 cup pine nuts

2/3 cups organic whole wheat bread crumbs (or substitute a gluten-free whole grain like spelt bread crumbs)

1 15oz. can organic navy beans, drained and rinsed (or cook your own)

2 organic omega-3 free-range eggs

2 tablespoons ground flaxseed meal

2 tablespoons ground chia seeds

1 tablespoon organic mustard

1 tablespoon organic tamari sauce (or soy sauce)

2 tablespoons 100% Moringa Oleifera (raw Powder Leaf) or spirulina

1/2 teaspoon fresh ground black pepper

2 fresh garlic buds (peeled)

have a bottle of organic olive oil handy

Directions

Add all the ingredients to a food processor. Pulse 15 times to combine.

(If you do not have a food processor, you can place all the ingredients to a zip lock bag and smash them together. Or: use a coffee grinder to grind the pine nuts into a flour before using and substitute garlic powder for fresh garlic and then everything will mix using a fork).

Chill mixed ingredients two hours or more.

Form into 4 patties.

In frying pan, cook in enough organic olive oil to cover the bottom of pan for 5 minutes on each side, turning every 2-3 minutes to make sure they do not burn, over medium-low heat.

Serve with your favorite toppings—ketchup, mustard, tomato, lettuce, sautéed onions—as a burger in a bun or melt some almond cheese on top and serve as side meat dish with your favorite vegetables.

We like to double the recipe and freeze some for future meals in the week. Also, each nut burger breaks up as a nice topping on pizza, over pasta, and in other dishes calling for meat toppings.

࿇

Elfin Hot Veggie Sandwiches

This recipe has been in the family ever since we moved to California and started regularly eating sprouts. It is delicious hot or cold, although we prefer it hot.

Ingredients

2 organic whole wheat pita bread rounds (you can also use any other flat bread)

2 large tomatoes (chopped in small pieces)

cup of alfalfa or clover sprouts

1 large avocado (or two small) peeled and cut in slices

½ cup of sliced (shitake) mushrooms

½ cup thinly sliced organic red bell peppers

1 small onion (chopped in small pieces)

1 cup of grated medium sharp non-GMO cheese, almond cheese, or goat cheese

Directions

Sauté the peppers, onions, tomatoes, and mushrooms in 2 tablespoons olive oil. Drain sautéed vegetables.

Cut pita bread rounds in half and stuff pocket with sautéed vegetables, cheese, then avocado, and then sprouts. Add a dribble of your favorite salad dressing into the sandwich before adding sprouts. Season with salt and pepper on top.

In frying pan, heat 2 tablespoons olive oil and on low heat, cook sandwich, flipping after 2 minutes on each side, until cheese has completely melted.

If you decide to eat this sandwich cold, we suggest you add with the veggies a small amount of thinly sliced dill pickle. This sandwich can be made with tortillas, but you must roll the ingredients inside and cook in the roll. Just be sure and do not over stuff it or it will fall apart.

Wild Pixies Wild Rice Stuffed Peppers

Wild Rice is heart healthy as it is high in Omega-3 and protein and does not contain gluten like other rice. Many people make stuffed peppers using ground beef and the following is actually a recipe we altered from a stuffed peppers recipe on the internet that called for beef, which we eliminated and added vegetable garden burger instead to go with our vegetarian choice. We also changed a number of the ingredients to healthy oils and produce. If you need to eat meat, then you may wish to add a half-pound of turkey burger to add flavor and protein. Chopped turkey sausage is also excellent in this recipe, as well as ground free-range bison.

(Preheat oven to 325 degrees)

(Serves 6, each person gets one half stuffed pepper)

Ingredients

3 organic green or red bell peppers

1 tablespoon olive oil

1/4 cup chopped onion

1/4 cup chopped organic celery

1/2 can (14.5 ounce can) diced tomatoes

1/2 can (8 ounce can) tomato sauce

1/2 teaspoon dried leaf organic oregano

pinch of Himalayan salt

small amount of ground black pepper

1 small lightly beaten

1 teaspoons organic Worcestershire sauce or
     tamari sauce (we like both)

6 small nut burgers or 4 large ones,
     cooked and chopped in small pieces

2 cups cooked wild rice

Directions

1. Add all ingredients together in small mixing bowl.

2. Cut tops off peppers and slice peppers in half. Remove most seeds. Rinse peppers well. Chop the edible part of pepper tops and set aside to use later. Place peppers in a large pot and cover with filtered water. Bring to a boil and then cover and turn to simmer for 5 minutes. Drain the peppers and set aside.

3. Heat olive oil in a large frying pan over medium heat. Sauté chopped green pepper (cuttings from the tops) and the chopped celery and onion for about 4 minutes, until tender. Add tomato sauce, tomatoes, spices, salt, and pepper. Simmer for about 8 minutes.

4. In a large mixing bowl, combine egg with Worcestershire or tamari sauce. Gently stir to blend and add diced nut burgers (see recipe previous in this chapter), cooked rice, and 1/2 cup of the simmered tomato mixture and stir, mixing completely.

5. Now, with halves of peppers turned up on back (forming a cup), stuff each with burger and tomato mixture and place in a 1 and 1/2 quart baking casserole glass or ceramic dish. Pour remaining tomato mixture over the stuffed peppers. Bake at 325°

for 35 to 45 minutes.

(Optional: For added protein, sprinkle stuffed peppers with a shredded almond cheese just before peppers are done; bake until cheese is melted. We also like to sprinkle on top of each burger some 100% pure Moringa Oleifera or some spirulina for extra protein and amino acids).

Hot Almond Butter Sandwiches

Here is an easy lunch! First make your sandwich using a liberal amount of organic almond butter inside 2 pieces of toasted homemade raisin bread (just use your toaster) or toasted sprouted grain Ezekiel Sesame bread (their raisin bread is also wonderful). Also spread as an inside topping some blueberry jam made from the recipe in chapter 9 (or a real fruit with no added sweetener you have bought).

Get ready a low heat frying pan with 2 tablespoons organic real butter melted. Place the sandwich in the pan and fry on each side for 1 minute or golden brown, cover to keep warm up.

Serve with sliced apples or other fresh fruit.

Elfin Mystic Pesto Pasta and Veggies

One of our favorite dinners is pesto pasta laying on a bed of fresh organic spinach leaves with an assortment of steamed veggies on top— zucchini, broccoli, shitake mushrooms and sliced tomatoes.

Just cook your favorite pasta and add to each cup of cooked pasta 2 tablespoons of homemade pesto from chapter 8. You can add more if you like, just taste it and add it to your liking. Also add more salt if you need.

Lay a half a cup of fresh organic spinach leaves on a plate. Spoon over that one cup of pesto pasta and add as a topping your favorite steamed vegetables. You can also sprinkle a bit of flax seed meal on top and a few added pine nuts with an extra tablespoon of pesto.

> Health Hint! It is important to eat spinach leaves raw, as cooking them turns it more into an acidic food. Fresh raw spinach, however, is more alkaline and is also heart healthy, assisting in keeping artery walls clear of cholesterol build-up.

Organic Corn on the Cob

Shuck and wash the ear of fresh corn (be sure it is organic and non-GMO). Slightly wet a paper towel. Wrap the ear of corn in the moist towel, and place on a microwavable plate. Cook in the microwave for 5 minutes. Remove the paper and serve.

Dwarves' Veggie Chili Soup
Ingredients

1 can organic white navy beans (15 oz.)

1 can organic red kidney beans (15 oz.)

1 can organic tomatoes (prefer with green chili peppers but peppers are optional)

1 fresh ears organic non-GMO sweet corn, microwaved

1 can mushroom- vegetable broth (15 oz.)

½ chopped onion

3 teaspoons chili powder

½ teaspoon minced fresh garlic

¼ teaspoon red pepper, crushed (optional)

4 grinds of fresh pepper

¼ cup low-fat Greek yogurt

Directions

Microwave the ears of corn (see previous

recipe). Shuck and cut off the kernels and place in a bowl. Drain beans. In a saucepan (large), mix all the ingredients together, including corn, except forthe yogurt. On low heat, simmer with lid on for about 20 minutes.

Serve in bowls and place a tablespoon of yogurt over each serving. You may also like to garnish with ½ tablespoon of chopped chives. Serves 4.

Elf Island Baken Beans

(Preheat oven to 300 degrees)

Ingredients:

2 and 1/3 cups dried white navy beans

Fresh filtered water for soaking beans

Vegetable stock broth, 2 cups

1 medium onion, diced

1 teaspoon garlic powder

1 medium organic red pepper, diced

½ cup black strap molasses unsulphured

1 tablespoon organic Worcestershire sauce

½ cup organic raw agave

pinch of salt

1 can of organic tomato sauce

1/3 cup organic mustard

¼ cup organic ketchup

Directions

First wash 2 and 1/3 cups (about a pound) of dried white navy beans in a colander. Soak the beans overnight in a medium pan covered with about 3 inches of water. Then drain off the water and wash the beans again.

Next place the beans in a 2-1/2-quart casserole dish and add the remaining ingredients. Stir a minute.

Cover (use aluminum foil if your casserole dish does not have a lid) and cook at 300 degrees for 3 hours.

Take them out of the oven and uncover. Taste and see if you need a little more salt and how done the beans are at this point.

You may wish to turn down the oven to 250 degrees and cook them a little off, this time without the cover to reduce the liquid. Some people who like them thick will cook them 3 more hours. We find usually 1 more hour is enough. Enjoy Elf Island Baken Beans!

Awaken now ye elven soul

Your spirit be forever whole!

Your Own Notes and Spells Go Here:

_____

_____

_____

_____

_____

_____

_____

_____

_____

_____

_____

_____

_____

_____

_____

_____

_____

_____

_____

_____

_____

_____

Chapter 8:
Soups, Salads, and Magical Side Dishes

Elfish Minestrone Soup

Ingredients

1 can of organic navy beans

1 can of organic red beans

1 medium onion finely diced

2 small garlic cloves fined diced

2 Tbs. (32 oz.) of organic vegetable broth

1 cup organic fresh green beans (cut small)

1 cup of organic zucchini (dice in small pieces)

1 large organic potato (peeled and diced in small pieces)

1 cup organic carrots (diced in small pieces)

2 cups filtered water

organic olive oil to use to sauté vegetables

1 teaspoon fresh thyme (dried is okay, too)

¼ teaspoon fresh oregano (dried is okay, too)

a few grinds of fresh black pepper

a couple of dashes of Himalayan or sea salt

1 cup organic whole wheat small or
   alphabet size noodles (cooked)

Steps for Making Minestrone Soup

Sauté onions and garlic in a little olive oil. Combine all other ingredients in a large (gallon) cooking pot except the noodles and bring to a boil. Turn heat to a slow boil and let it cook about 8 minutes until squash and potatoes are cooked and soft. Add cooked noodles. Turn to low heat and simmer for about 10 more minutes. Turn off heat and let it cool down. Then refrigerate in containers. This can even be frozen for later use in individual covered freezer containers. This soup is better the second day after it has had a day for the ingredients to combine flavors.

Good Folk's Lentil Soup
Ingredients:

1 cup dried organic lentils

½ cup organic whole grain uncooked rice

2 pinches of Himalayan salt

a few grinds of black pepper

¼ cup organic olive oil

1 onion (chopped into small pieces)

Directions:

Sauté chopped onion in olive oil. While onion is cooking, wash the lentils and low boil them in saucepan (takes about 10 minutes). Add the onions to the lentils. Now add the rice and more water (should be above the lentils). Cook for about 30 more minutes (add water as needed). Test taste the rice and make sure it is tender. The beans and rice will have absorbed the water. Add the salt and pepper. We like to serve it hot with sprinkles of finely chopped chives.

Water Nympths' Coconut Milk Soup

Ingredients

2 cups of vegetable stock (save water from cooking vegetables)

½ cup fresh shitake mushrooms, sliced thin

2 cans of organic coconut milk (13.5 ounces)

2 tablespoon fresh lime juice

3 teaspoons red curry paste

1 stalk lemon grass (minced)

1/3 cup chopped cilantro

1 tablespoon raw agave

3 grinds of pepper

1 garlic bud minced

1 tablespoon fresh grated ginger

2 tablespoons onion cut in very small pieces

½ cup fresh organic spinach

1 pound cooked fresh shrimp if you can find
   clean water shrimp (otherwise substitute
   your favorite white fish)

3 tablespoons organic Worcestershire sauce
   (or fish sauce)

Directions

In hot frying pan, cook 1 minute in a tablespoon of olive oil the curry paste, lemon grass, ginger, onion, and garlic. Stir in the vegetable stock, agave and Worcestershire sauce. Keep stirring a minute then cook on low heat for 10 minutes. Next add coconut milk and mushrooms. Cook until mushrooms are soft. Add shrimp and cook 5 more minutes (or until shrimp are no longer translucent). Stir in lime juice and salt and fresh spinach and cook 2 more minutes.

Serve in bowls and garnish with cilantro.

Elven Miso soup

Ingredients

4 cups filtered water or try 3 cups filtered

water and 1 cup coconut milk

4 tablespoons yellow miso paste

2 teaspoons dashi granules

8 ounces silken tofu, diced

2 green onions sliced in diagonal ½ inch pieces

½ cup dried Wakame sea vegetables

¼ cup chopped organic kale

Directions:

First soak sea vegetables in 2 cups cold filtered water for 5 minutes. Then remove from water (save water) and slice in small pieces.

In a saucepan over medium to high heat,

combine the dashi granules and remaining 2 cups water saved from soaking sea vegetables and 2 more cups (to make 4 altogether) and bring to a boil. Reduce heat to low-medium, and add in the miso paste. Stir in the tofu pieces. Add the green onion, kale, and sea vegetables. Simmer gently for 2 to 3 minutes before serving. Enough for 4 servings and will store in refrigerator.

(We often do not have the dashi and just use filtered water. It is still delicious, but always using dashi is the traditional Japanese method of making miso.)

Menehune Papaya Salad

Ingredients

1 Papaya peeled and cut in small pieces

one small head of green lettuce cut up

1 cup organic fresh spinach

And ingredients for the dressing:

1 tablespoon organic olive oil

1 tablespoon balsamic vinegar

1 tablespoon organic lemon juice

Directions

Toss papaya and spinach together in a large salad bowl. Mix the 3 ingredients for the dressing in a cup and it pour evenly over salad. Toss well. Sprinkle a couple of pinches of Himalayan salt over the salad and a couple of grinds of fresh pepper. Serve chilled!

Magic Cold Salad Green Beans

Ingredients

1pound washed green beans (without stems)

1 glove of garlic

¼ cup of organic olive oil

fresh ground pepper

a couple of dashes of Himalayan salt

4 teaspoons of apple cider vinegar

1 tablespoon of organic Dijon mustard

Directions

Prep Day Before Serving:

1. Prepare a bowl of water with ice cubes that is large enough to hold the green beans after they are cooked. Set this aside.

2. Next, steam the washed green beans (with whole peeled garlic placed on top) until tender (about 5 minutes). Take out the garlic and place the green beans in the ice water. When the beans are cool, drain them and pat them dry.

3. Make a vinaigrette by mashing the garlic into a paste and place in a small bowl, add oil and apple cider vinegar and mustard and stir well.

4. Set beans and vinaigrette aside in separate bowls to cool in the refrigerator for over night (at least 8 hours).

On Serving Day:

Right before serving, toss the green beans and vinaigrette together and then enjoy!

Brownies' Pumpkin and Raisin Soufflé

This is a very quick and easy side dish that adds nutritionally to almost any meal, particularly good one to add along with other vegetables. We love it!

Use a small glass casserole dish that will go in your microwave. Spoon one can (15 oz.) of pure organic canned pumpkin in the dish. Add four omega-3 organic eggs. Add a tablespoon of cinnamon and a little vanilla. Add ¼ cup raw organic agave (add more or less to your taste) and 2 tablespoons of black strap molasses. Stir in ¼ cup of organic raisins and ¼ cup of walnuts. Add 4 tablespoons almond milk. Whip well. Microwave for about 5 minutes. Watch for the middle to change from a liquid to more like a pudding. Serve hot as side vegetable.

Refrigerate leftovers: is good the next day cold or reheated.

Elfin Mango Rice

Ingredients

1 tablespoon organic olive oil

½ cup chopped organic celery

¼ cup chopped green onion

2 cups hot cooked organic brown rice

2 cups of fresh chopped mango slices

dash of Himalayan salt

¼ teaspoon curry powder

¼ teaspoon ground ginger

Directions:

Sauté celery and green onions in olive oil in a

large frying pan. Stir in the cooked rice, chopped mango, curry, salt and ginger. Cover and cook over low heat for 6 minutes or until completely heated. Transfer to serving plate and add a garnish of parsley, if you like. Makes about 5-6 servings.

Elfin Green Salad Delight

Nearly every night, we eat a green salad and try to get as many super foods in our salads as possible.

Ingredients

2 cups cut salad greens (organic baby

spinach, along with organic green leaf

and/or romaine lettuce)

¼ cup organic green kale, chopped

¼ cup thinly sliced purple or green cabbage

¼ cup thinly sliced radishes

¼ cup alfalfa or clover sprouts

¼ cup sliced organic cucumbers

2 tablespoons finely chopped chives

2 tablespoons of pine nuts

1 teaspoon ground flax and 1 teaspoon

ground organic chia seeds

(optional) ½ cup of raw pickled veggies (fermented) of your choice, our favorites are cauliflower, zucchini, and eggplant (considered a healthy delicacy in northern Japan).

Directions

Place fresh greens and cabbage, radishes, cucumbers, and sprouts in a large salad bowl. Sprinkle chives evenly on top, then chia and flax meal. We like to put on the salad dressing before adding the final topping of sprouts and pickled veggies.

We also like to alternate super food ingredients in our salads each night, so some nights we add chopped fresh beets and avocado chunks instead of radishes and pine nuts. Or we may also add blueberries or raspberries instead of radishes and chives, and arugula instead of cabbage. Papaya is also delicious and blends well in the palate with almost all veggies (except perhaps onions and chives). Walnuts are heart healthy and also delicious in salads, and they go well with all veggies and fruit. We like to eat mostly pine nuts, however, for their alkaline content.

ॐ

Eternity Oatmeal

This recipe is altered just a bit from the delicious breakfast recipe that Silver Flame's colleague and friend Robert W Sterling (Bob) of over 40 years, told her at one point when he was a spry 94 years old. He was still cooking every morning for himself. Oatmeal has long been purported as a hearty food many people think gives them abundant energy and longevity. We tried his recipe and love it too!

Ingredients

½ cup organic whole grain rolled oats

1 cup non-fat milk (Bob likes to use whole milk but we use organic non-fat milk or almond milk)

1/4 tablespoon organic Pumpkin Pie Seasoning (or include an even mixture of your own organic cinnamon, ginger, nutmeg, allspice and cloves.)

2 heaping tablespoon of organic almond nut butter (crunchy if you can find it) or crunchy peanut butter

1 heaping tablespoon of fruit jelly, sweetened only with fruit juice (or try making and using the blueberry jelly in chapter 9

that is sweetened with raw agave).

two dashes of Himalayan salt

Directions

Heat the above ingredients except the oatmeal to first signs of boiling, stirring constantly to avoid milk scum from forming. Add (sprinkle) the oatmeal, to avoid lumping. Stir constantly until thickening occurs to your likening. The whole process takes about 5 minutes.

Elven Air Corps Jetlag Fruit Cocktail

The next time you are jetlagged, try eating this to help you naturally produce melatonin that regulates your sleep:

Mix equal amounts of unsweetened fresh pineapple chunks, slices of bananas, and cut orange slices (no rinds) together. Pour 2 tablespoons of fresh orange juice over each serving to moisten. (optional: Sprinkle ¼ teaspoon of grated orange zest on top.)

A bit of that

A pinch of this

Will lead in time

To total bliss!

Your Own Notes and Spells Go Here:

_____

_____

_____

_____

_____

_____

_____

_____

_____

_____

_____

_____

_____

_____

_____

_____

_____

_____

Chapter 9:
Elvish Condiments and Sauces

Homemade Organic Ketchup

Ingredients

1 can (6 once) organic tomato paste

¼ cup organic balsamic vinegar

1 tablespoons organic raw agave

1 teaspoon organic black strap molasses

½ tablespoon garlic powder or onion

    powder (optional)

1/8 teaspoon allspice (optional)

dash of Himalayan salt

1 cup filtered water

Directions

Mix all the ingredients together except the water. After everything is well mixed, add water and continue to mix well. Refrigerate in glass jar or refrigerator airtight container and it is ready to use.

Green Heaven Greek-Yogurt Dressing

Ingredients

½ cup olive oil

¼ cup organic balsamic vinegar

¼ cup organic apple cider vinegar

2 teaspoons lemon juice

¼ cup filtered water

2 teaspoons sesame seed oil

1 tablespoon soy sauce or tamari sauce

½ cup Greek low-fat yogurt

1 tablespoon kelp powder

½ teaspoon garlic powder

½ teaspoon ground ginger

dash of fresh ground black pepper

3 tablespoons of organic liquid chlorophyll

1 tablespoon finely ground chia seeds

1 tablespoon finely ground flax seeds

Directions

Mix all the ingredients (wet first then dry) together except the water. After everything else is mixed, add water and stir. Enjoy using on salads and as a sauce on cooked vegetables too. We love this on

156   The Silver Elves

steamed broccoli. If you are using this as a salad dressing, you may wish to thin it down and add another ¼ cup of water. Also, use one of your tasting spoons and adjust amounts of spices to your own taste. We often add a little extra ginger.

Mer Folk Yogurt Tartar Sauce

Ingredients

1/2 cup plain yogurt

2-3 tablespoons dill pickle relish or chop

 them yourself

2 tablespoons chopped chives

1 teaspoon organic lemon juice

2 teaspoon organic Dijon mustard

dash of Worcestershire sauce

salt and pepper to taste

(adding a couple of tablespoons of capers is

optional)

Directions:

Mix all ingredients together and place in refrigerator for at least one hour before using. Great to use on oven baked fish!

Bluebell's Blueberry Jelly

Ingredients

3 cups organic blueberries (or cranberries)

3 tablespoons organic raw agave (2 more for cranberries)

¼ cup filtered water or coconut water

2 tablespoons organic lemon juice

2 to 4 tablespoons arrowroot powder

Directions

First add the arrowroot in the clean cup. Next, add about 3 tablespoons of the water to the arrowroot and stir it up. Arrowroot needs to dissolve in cool or room temperature water before adding to a mixture on the stove. In a boiling pan, combine all other ingredients including the remainder of the water. Cook slowly until berries are well cooked. Add arrowroot mixture and stir well. Cook until it is like a jelly consistency. Pour into a clean container for storage and refrigerate. You can use it in just a couple of hours once it chills.

~

Visionary Raw Cocoa Syrup

Ingredients

½ cups filtered water or coconut water

½ to ¾ cup organic raw agave (we like less sweetening but you may like adding the extra ¼ cup, taste as you go)

½ cup raw organic cocoa powder

dash of Himalayan sea salt

1 teaspoon vanilla extract

Directions

Combine the water, agave, raw cocoa powder, and salt together in a saucepan over low heat. Stir constantly until the mixture thickens a little on low boil for a couple of minutes. Remove from heat and stir the vanilla into the sauce. Serve warm or cover and refrigerate until serving. If you refrigerate, it will thicken. Great as a dessert topping, use sparingly.

Elfin Mint Sauce

Blend 1 cup of fresh mint (no stems), one peeled clove of garlic, with 2 cups of organic Greek yogurt. Add one chopped small green bell pepper, ½ teaspoon Himalayan salt, and 2 tablespoons fresh lemon juice. Blend. You can also add 1 tablespoon liquid chlorophyll for extra nutrient density. If you do not have enough mint, parsley works well too so mix and match!

Basal and Pine Nut Pesto
Ingredients

½ cup pine nuts (or walnuts or half and half)

6 cloves of chopped garlic

4 cups fresh basal leaves

1 cup of organic olive oil

1 tablespoons of organic chlorophyll (or however much you can get away with putting in without your family and guests objecting)

1 cup grated parmesan cheese (raw if possible)

½ teaspoon Himalayan salt

4 grinds of fresh pepper

Directions

Place nuts and garlic in food processor or blender and process for about 20 seconds. Add basal leaves, salt and pepper, and pour in olive oil and chlorophyll and process as you pour. Continue processing until completely mixed and pureed. Add the cheese and puree for one more minute.

This makes an excellent salad dressing or use with cooked noodles to make pesto pasta.

Dreamy Fresh Fruit Yogurt Dip

Ingredients

Ingredients for dip:

8 oz. of organic low-fat Greek yogurt

¼ cup unsweetened organic applesauce

1 tablespoon organic raw agave

1/8 teaspoon ground organic cinnamon

1/8 teaspoon ground ginger

1 teaspoon vanilla

Fruit: 3 cups of sliced fresh fruit (assortment of pineapple chunks, mangoes, papayas, strawberries, apples, and peaches)

Directions

In a small bowl, combine the dip ingredients. Place and spear fruit on a plate with toothpicks. Serve dip bowl and fruit on the same plate. Dip fruit into yogurt mix.

෯

Stirring round

This spell is made

True love will come

And never fade!

Your Own Notes and Spells Go Here:

_____

_____

_____

_____

_____

_____

_____

_____

_____

_____

_____

Chapter 10:
The Happy Gut and Healthy Heart

The Happy Gut

Much has been researched these days about the importance of having healthy flora in the gut and how this affects both physical and mental health. Research at UCLA, for instance, has shown in a population of women that eating foods like yogurt with probiotics can help fight depression and stress.

For some time, scientists have understood how the head affects the gut in development. As early as the 1830's, William Beaumont, an army surgeon who is known now as the "Father of Gastric Physiology", found an association between changing moods and gastric secretions. The classical view of top-down control with the brain's ability to control gut function has been supported by evidence revealing that the brain influences body systems, like the gastro intestinal tract, particularly when the person is under stress. Now there is new evidence to show also a bottom-up control with the gut, the microbiota in the gastro-intestinal tract, can influence brain functioning and is linked to behavior, depression, stress, and stress-related diseases. Neuroscientists are now evaluating the role of gut microbiota modulation on emotional processing in the brain and its functioning. This "good" bacteria, the "good" flora in your gut, may be instrumental in how your brain develops, you behave, and react to stress.

Here is a list of foods you may wish to add as much as possible into your diet to maintain a healthy balance of gut flora and assist in restoring a healthy balance in your intestinal tract: **raw apple cider vinegar, ginger, high fiber fruits and veggies, raw almonds, chia seeds, flax seed oil and meal, and fermented foods such as Greek yogurt, kefir, sauerkraut - pickled eggplant, pickled beets, pickled radishes, Korean Kimichi, Natto, miso, tempeh, and fermented tofu.**

For an excellent resource on how to pickle (ferment) your own vegetables for little cost see Dr. John Bergman's video on gut health and fermenting at: https://www.youtube.com/watch?v=TiigsFnNDuQ. It is a very easy process and can be done yourself for much less the price than buying fermented vegetables in health food stores. Using these veggies everyday in green salads and other vegetable dishes will increase your good gut bacteria and increase your immune system.

There is also much more you can do in addition to building up the good flora in your body to assure good gut health that effects positive mental health. Along with her colleague Robert Sterling, Silver Flame (writing as Martha Char Love) published a book available on Amazon titled *What's Behind Your Belly Button? A Psychological Perspective of the Intelligence of Human Nature and Gut Instinct*, on accessing gut feelings by using the Somatic Reflection Process that they developed. This process is one that helps you resolve emotional issues felt in the gut and unite your body-mind. The happier your gut is and the calmer it feels emotionally, the more positive signals will flow from your gut brain to your head brain, and your mental and physical health will be vastly improved. This process will also provide stress reduction that has positive effects upon one's physical body (surely including digestion) and assists the immune system in the elimination of dis-ease.

It seems sensible that if we have a feeling of tenseness in our gut, that is what people often call a gut knot, we are cutting off the flow of vitality from our gut that we depend upon for health and well-being. A wise doctor once said that "if your eyes can not cry, then your gut will". He was describing the reason your gut might be in pain physically in relation to emotional pain of which your head is in denial. Your head and even your heart may be in denial, but your gut can't be. That you can count on! Surely, all of us have had the experience of laughing or crying until our gut feels it. But if our thinking brain and our heart are in denial of our feelings and essential needs as living beings, our gut will cry or signal us (i.e. irritable bowel syndrome, stomach pains, dis-ease, etc) like a red flag to be aware of ourselves and our instinctual human needs of freedom and acceptance until our thinking brain gets the communication.

We have found that the Somatic Reflection Process on gut feelings is vital for improving the emotional immune system and mental health, as well as developing gut feeling awareness to follow in healthy decision-making. We recommend its use daily along with any probiotic diet plan to work hand-in-hand for digestion. Make your gut happy with both good bacteria and gut feeling awareness to send the maximum signals of happiness to the thinking brain, becoming whole as an elfin being.

Organic Edamame and Depression

All of us go through times of depression and cycles of low energy. We have all heard that eating a bit of 70% + dark chocolate is good for regulating mood because it releases endorphins in the brain and can boost serotonin levels (it contains compounds, like phenylethylamine, that act as mild stimulants). But it is less known that edamame has high levels of tryptophan, and soybeans also rank low on the glycemic index, so they don't spike energy levels too quickly that would cause a mood crash later.

Just a little over a cup of organic edamame (be sure they are 100% organic and no GMO) gives you 9 grams of fiber (about the same amount you'll find in 4 slices of whole-wheat bread or 4 cups of steamed zucchini). It has almost as much protein as it does carbohydrate. It contains around 10% of the Daily Value for two key antioxidants like vitamin C and A. And for a plant food, it's quite high in iron; it has about as much as a 4-ounce roasted chicken breast. Also, for depression, eat cashews and bananas for the high counts of tryptophan; and bananas are a potassium powerhouse as well.

Himalayan Salt

It is advisable to change from table salt to premium sea salts (table salt is fired at such high temperatures that it is not even recognized as salt to your body anymore and relatively unusable). We found a particularly good brand of Himalayan salt, SunFire, advertised in a book Silver Flame read by her author friend, Clint Evans called "Get Down to 150 - Finally, Healthy Natural Foods for Busy Women to Melt Fat Without Dieting or Insane Exercise so You Can Fit Into Those Skinny Jeans in 3 Simple Steps". We highly recommend his book for everyone because he has such great diet tips and explanations on the needs of the human body that are well researched but easy for anyone to understand. He suggests SunFire salt because many of the other brands of Himalayan salts still use cooper grinders. SunFire uses a stainless steal grinder.

Pristine SunFire Salt is a gourmet blend of 4 premium salts, made up of Bolivian Rose Salt, Himalayan Pink Salt, Hawaiian Alaea Clay Salt and Chinese Sea Salt from the original Ming Dynasty Saltworks, and at least at the time of writing of this book, must be bought on the internet. You get 2 pounds for $20, so that lasts a long time. See the following web address for ordering information:

http://lovingsuperfoods.com/rawfood/sunfiresalt.html

Try Eating Something New! Mangosteins, Durians, and Pear Apples!

You will surely find a few new-to-you food ingredients used in this book. While it is important to be cautious in eating any new foods and you may need to consult your health practitioner first, there is much to be said for trying new foods.

It may well be a good idea for longevity to try a new food every so often. When the body senses a new experience like eating something it has never tasted, it wakes up! Perhaps it opens up some new pathways in the brain and says "Hey, there are still new experiences to be had! Live on!" We realized this when we were visiting in Thailand and tasting some unknown-to-us-previously fruits (mangosteins, durians and pear apples) out of our friend's garden where we was staying in Bangkok. Zardoa said, "This is probably putting new things in our bodies that it has never had before and must be making us a new person in certain ways".

If we go a little outside our own cultural foods and explore the foods of others, we find a world of nurturing foods awaiting us. People who have various food allergies may feel limited in their diet, but often there is an abundance of food we are not allergic to that we simply have not tried, particularly from other cultures. So if you are cooking for someone in your family who is allergic to bananas, for instance, try some new fruits (of course consult your health practitioner first). Just be sure that you wash all fruits and vegetables quite well and if you are concerned about food hygiene, just eat the inside and leave the peel.

Food That Will Help You Regulate Your Sleep

Melatonin is a hormone produced by the pineal gland that controls your circadian sleeping-waking cycles. Jet lag and shift work can cause a disturbance in melatonin production and therefore cause difficulty in sleeping. (See the recipe for Elven Air Corps Jet Lag

Fruit Cocktail in chapter 8.) Researchers from Thailand's Khon Kaen University have found that the melatonin in the body can be naturally raised through eating certain tropical fruits, including:

Pineapples, Bananas, Oranges, Mangosteins, as well as other food like Oats, Sweet Corn, Rice, Barley, Ginger, and Tomatoes

Try eating some the next time your sleep cycle is off!

For the dishwasher:

As I scrub and make these clean

My life takes a whole new sheen!

Your Own Notes and Spells Go Here:

_____

_____

_____

_____

_____

_____

_____

_____

_____

_____

Chapter 11:
One for the Elf Hounds!
Puppy Pancake Treat

Here is one of our favorite dog treat recipes that we came up with after looking at a number of recipes on the internet and altering them to include bananas and blackstrap molasses and which our favorite elf dog loves:

(preheat oven to 350 degrees)

Ingredients:

1/4 cup mashed organic banana

1 tbsp. organic blackstrap molasses

2 tbsp. filtered water

1 tbsp. organic olive oil

1 cup organic whole wheat flour

1/8 tsp. baking soda

1/8 tsp. baking powder

Directions

Mix banana, molasses, olive oil, and water together in a bowl. Add the flour, baking soda, and baking powder. Stir until dough softens a bit.

With lightly wet hands, scoop a tablespoon into your hands and roll in a ball. Place the ball onto a lightly greased cookie sheet and press the ball down to flatten into pancake, only 1/8 inch in height. Repeat until sheet is filled.

This recipe makes about three cookie sheets worth or four dozen.

(Optional) Before baking, press a cookie cutter into the center of each to indent a cute shape in each treat.

Bake approximately 22 minutes, (25 minutes for crunchier).

(As an alternative treat, try using canned pumpkin or fresh creamed sweet potatoes instead of bananas and 2 tablespoons molasses instead of just 1)

Hint: If you like this dog treat recipe and would like more wonderful original recipes, look for Silver Flame's (Martha Char Love) dog treat book, co-authored with Rosemary "Mamie" and Doug Adkins, and Linda Hales, titled *Maggie's Kitchen Tails*, to be released in the Fall of 2015, with 20% profits donated to dog abuse rescue.

Chapter 12:
Non-Toxic Kitchen Cleaning Tips

Cleaning Your Oven Using Non-Toxic Household Products

You Need:

> A Spray Bottle with a Mixture of 1/3 Vinegar and 2/3 Water
>
> Baking Soda
>
> Coarse Salt (we use Hawaiian Salt)

Remove the oven racks (clean these separately with same method). Now, spray the entire oven including the inside of the oven door with the vinegar mixture, making it wet all over. Sprinkle baking soda everywhere inside the oven and on the door, applying more on areas where food is built up. Sprinkle a thick layer of salt over the baking soda. Then spray again with the vinegar mixture. It will fizz and bubble. Let it sit overnight. Scrub the oven with a scouring pad or sponge (rough surface). All the caked food will come up easily. Spray again with the vinegar mixture to help remove any food left. Wipe with paper towels.

Cleaning the Food Smells from Inside Your Microwave

If your microwave oven has a food odor coming from it when you open the door, wipe it clean with sponge and wash the turn-around. While the turn-around is still out of the oven, use either fresh or bottled pure lemon juice (does not need to be organic) to wipe the insides of the microwave from top to bottom. The lemon juice will both clean and freshen it up and get rid of the smell of food left from previous use.

Cleaning Sterling (Elven) Silver

Whether it is your sterling silverware or dishes, you may dread using them because you hate using the toxic cleaners on the market for sterling silver. Well, no more worries! Use any common toothpaste brand as a cleaner. Rub a generous amount all over the piece you are cleaning and let it sit for an hour. Then with a soft cloth, rub it gently. You will notice that the cloth turns black. When you are finished, rinse the sterling elf ware in warm water to get the toothpaste completely off and then dry it with a kitchen towel. Repeat if necessary. If the toothpaste is hard to get off an area, use a soft toothbrush instead of the cloth. (This method also works well for your sterling rings, necklaces and bracelets).

174   The Silver Elves

Appendix 1:
ANDI Scores

Check the ANDI scores below of your food ingredients (listed from highest to lowest in nutrient density):

1. Kale — 1000 (ANDI Score)
2. Collard/Mustard/Turnip Greens — 1000
3. Watercress — 1000
4. Bok Choy and Baby Bok Choy — 824
5. Spinach — 739
6. Broccoli Rabe (rapini) — 715
7. Chinese/Napa Cabbage — 704
8. Brussels Sprouts — 672
9. Swiss Chard — 670
10. Arugula — 559
11. Radish — 554
12. Cabbage — 481
13. Bean Sprouts — 444
14. Romaine Lettuce — 389
15. Broccoli — 376
16. Red Pepper — 366
17. Turnip — 337
18. Carrot Juice — 344
19. Carrot — 336
20. Cauliflower —295
21. Artichoke — 244
22. Strawberries — 212
23. Pomegranate Juice —193
24. Tomato —190
25. Blackberries — 178
26. Plum —157
27. Butternut Squash — 156
28. Raspberries — 145

29. Blueberries — 130
30. Orange —109
31. Lentils — 104
32. Cantaloupe — 100
33. Red Kidney Beans — 100
34. Kiwi — 97
35. Northern Beans — 94
36. Watermelon — 91
37. Black Beans — 83
38. Sunflower Seeds — 78
39. Peach — 73
40. Apple — 72
41. Cherries — 68
42. Sesame Seeds — 65
43. Flax Seeds — 65
44. Pineapple — 64
45. Apricot— 60
46. Edamame — 58
47. Chickpeas (Garbanzo Beans) — 57
48. Pumpkin Seeds — 52
49. Pistachios — 48
50. Pecans — 41
51. Almonds — 38
52. Tofu — 37
53. Walnuts— 34
54. Cashews — 27
55. White potato — 31
56. Banana—30

The scores above are suggested by Dr. Joel Furhman (see his book *Eat for Health*) who created the Aggregate Nutrient Density Index or the ANDI, a score assigned to whole foods that contain the highest nutrients per calorie and are the foods from which our bodies are able to absorb and utilize the most nutrients.

Appendix 2:
pH Levels of Ingredients of the Recipes in This Book: Accentuate the Alkaline in Your Diet

Many of the following ingredients in these first two charts of alkaline foods are used in the recipes in this book and are considered alkaline by many authorities (although experts do differ widely in their opinions on this). We suggest that you do your own research. We try to eat as much as possible from the first "very alkaline" and also from the second "moderate to low alkaline" food charts to be sure the diet is more alkaline! It is advised to use alkaline foods in your diet 3 to 5 times more than acidic ingredients (this includes drinks):

Chart 1

Very Alkaline (produce a significantly high alkaline ash when metabolized)	
Alfalfa Grass	Miso
Apricots	Onions
Baking Soda	Oranges
Beets	Potato Skins
Broccoli	Pumpkin

Celery	Pumpkin Seeds
Cucumbers	Radish
Currants	Seed Sprouts (i.e. Clover)
Figs	**Spinach** (uncooked)
Grapefruits	Tangerines
(Very Alkaline continued)	**Umeboshi** (Japanese Plum)
Kale	Wheat Grass
Lemon Water (Fresh Lemon)	
Lemons (Fresh)	
Limes (Fresh)	

Chart 2

Alkaline or Slightly Alkaline (produce a moderate to low alkaline ash when metabolized)	
Almonds	Garlic
Almond Milk	Ghee
Apple Cider Vinegar	Ginger (fresh or root)
Apples	Ginseng
Arugula	Green Cabbage
Avocado	Green Beans
Avocado Oil	Green Tea
Bean Sprouts	Himalayan Salt
Bell Peppers	Kombucha
Blackberries	Kombu (sea vegetables)
Blueberries	Kiwi
Bok Choy and Baby Bok Choy	Mangoes
Broccoli	Millet
Brown Rice (organic only, very low alkaline)	Molasses (Blackstrap Unsulfured**)**
Brussels Sprouts	Mushrooms
Buckwheat	Mustard Greens
Butter Milk	Nori (Seaweed)
Butternut Squash	Olives
	Olive Oil (Virgin, Cold Pressed)

Cabbage	Oregano (Fresh is best)
Carrots	Papaya
Chard	Parsley
Cauliflower	Peaches
Celery	Peas
Chestnuts	Pineapples
Chia Seeds	Pine Nuts
Chives	Pomegranate Juice
Cherries	Potatoes (organic with skins)
Cinnamon	Plums
Coconut Oil	Quinoa
Dates	Raisins
Edamame	Raspberries
Flax Seeds	Reishi Mushrooms (one of more alkaline mushrooms)
Rice Syrup	Whole Wheat (Organic only, very low alkaline)
Romaine Lettuce	Yams
Sake	Zucchini
Sesame Seeds	
Sesame Seed Oil	
Shitake Mushrooms (one of the more alkaline mushrooms)	
Soy Sauce (naturally fervented)	
Spelt	
Spiralina	
Sprouted Grains	
Strawberries	
Tofu	
Tomatoes (fresh not canned)	
Wakame (brown seawed)	
Watermelon	
Water	
Wild rice	

Chart 3

Lowest in Acid Level of Acidic Foods It is suggested that one eats sparingly from these lowest in acid forming levels of the acidic foods. Eat no more than 1/3 of total diet from these foods or 1/3 of ingredients in a recipe (many experts suggest a higher alkaline 5 to 1 ratio). If your recipe exceeds the alkaline-acidic ratio of 3-1 in acidic food levels, then be sure that your overall diet that day compensates. It is more difficult than one would think to recover from eating or drinking highly acid forming foods, so we suggest you try not to eat or drink food that is higher in acidic levels than the ones listed below:

Agave (raw and organic)	Venison
Butter	Whole Milk
Chicken Eggs	
Cranberries	
Curry	
Duck (Wild)	
Fish	
Greek Yogurt (Lowfat)	
Honey	
Stevia (Vanilla)	

These charts are information compiled from a number of sources including the Toronto Public Health, Dr. Jacquilen Tomas-Ali, ND viewed on http://beatcancer.org, *Mayo Clinic Diet Manual*, 7th Edition, and *The Acid Alkaline Food Guide: A Quick Reference to Foods & Their Effect on pH Levels*. Because experts do not agree on whether many foods are alkaline or acidic, we suggest that you do your own research and make your own list according to your own findings and how your body reacts. We use pH paper testing of both urine and saliva early morning to determine if our choices of food has truly balanced our pH levels and that is the true guide you need for determining what foods you should eat and not eat.

Appendix 3:
Guide to Measurement Substitutions

Weights and measures for cooking contributed by Silver Flame's beloved mother, Martha Campbell Whitenton:

1 tablespoon = 3 teaspoons
1 ounce of liquid = 2 tablespoons
1 cup = 8 oz. of liquids = 16 tablespoons = 237 ml
3/4 cup = 6 oz. = 12 tablespoons = 177 ml
2/3 cup = 5 oz. = 11 tablespoons = 158 ml
1/2 cup = 4 oz. = 8 tablespoons = 118 ml
1/3 cup = 3 oz. = 5 and 1/3 tablespoons = 79 ml
1/4 cup = 2 oz. = 4 tablespoons = 59 ml
1/8 cup = 1 oz. = 2 tablespoons = 30 ml
2 cups = 1 pt.
4 cups = 1 quart
4 quarts = 1 gallon
8 quarts = 1 peck
4 pecks = 1 bushel
1 lb liquid = 16 ounces
1 lb (pound) flour = about 4 cups
1 lb rice = 2 cups
1 lb cheese = 5 cups (grated)
1 square chocolate bitter = 1 ounce
3 tablespoons cocoa powder = 1 square chocolate

Filled with life you'll surely be

When you taste this recipe

Your Own Notes and Spells Go Here:

_____

_____

_____

_____

_____

_____

_____

_____

_____

_____

_____

_____

_____

_____

_____

_____

_____

_____

_____

About the Authors

The Silver Elves are retired in Oahu, Hawaii, and have been working to complete this book of healthy foods to assist people working on goals for excellent gut health and positive wellbeing. We did not write this cookbook as professional nutritionists but more as parents and lifetime family cooks who have always had the wellbeing of our family's health and happiness in mind. Silver Flame and Zardoa, like wizards and witches of olde, have a continuing interest in herbs, spices, concoctions and things that won't go bump in your intestines.

You will also find included in this book several original recipes from Silver Flame's own mother Martha Campbell Whitenton, who was one of the world's best family cooks. Before Martha Campbell Whitenton passed away in January of 2014, she was very excited that some of her original recipes would be included in this book and also that there would be a version of her recipes altered to include more healthy ingredients for a more nutritious meal. Martha Campbell Whitenton was a woman with a high regard and goals for advanced education of all people and who at one time was a professor of accounting at the same community college, Meridian Junior College, where Silver Flame was teaching psychology and was a full-time guidance counselor. Martha Campbell Whitenton always stressed to her family the importance of learning and making changes to meet one's full human potential. Her inspiring influence is the reason that Silver Flame was able to freely alter her recipes and invent these new gut and heart healthy meals. Silver Flame demonstrates how to honor your own mother's cooking by making her recipes healthier to meet today's nutritional knowledge and by altering them freely for your own wellbeing.

We would like to suggest that there is much more you can do for your digestive system along with eating the right foods. We encourage you to experience achieving body-mind unity through reducing stress using the Somatic Reflection Process to explore and understand your gut feeling responses and emphasizes that this is the key to calming the gut and having positive gut health. To learn the reflection process technique that will further increase your gut awareness and natural sense of well-being, please be sure and explore the blog site dedicated to the book What's Behind Your Belly Button? about gut feeling intelligence at http://instinctualgutfeelings.blogspot.com.

If you are interested in more of our books on Elven Philosophy, Lore and Magic check out our website at http://silverelves.angelfire.com and join us on Facebook, under the name Silver Elves.

Elven magic is a magic of Life, Liberty, and the Pursuit of Happiness with a liberal dash of poetic license.